45 Healthy Soul Food Recipes

Publications International, Ltd.

Favorite Brand Name Recipes at www.fbnr.com

American Heart Association Team: Linda Ball, Deborah Renza, Barthy Gaitonde, Janice Moss, Jackie Haigney, Robin Sullivan, and Michelle Overcash

Recipe Developers: Maurietta Amos, Jennifer Booker, Nancy S. Hughes, Annie King, Carol Ritchie, and Julie Shapero, R.D., L.D.

Recipe Analyst: Tammi Hancock, R.D.

Front cover/back cover photography and photography on pages 9, 13, 15, 17, 19, 23, 27, 31, 33, 37, 39, 41, 43, 47, 49, 51, 53, 55, 59, 63, 65, 67, 71, 73 and 75 by Chris Cassidy Photography

Photographer: Chris Cassidy
Photographer's Assistant: Brian Fogle
Prop Stylist: Nancy Cassidy
Food Stylists: David Kennedy, Carol Smoler
Assistant Food Stylist: Christina Zerkis

Pictured on the front cover: Spicy Oven-Fried Chicken *(page 30)*
Pictured on the back cover: Shrimp Gumbo *(page 26)*

Portraits Photography: Fuchs and Kasperek Photography, Cleveland, Ohio *(page 89)*; Jason Allen Norman Photography, Mobile, Alabama *(page 91)*

ISBN-13: 978-1-4127-2651-1
ISBN-10: 1-4127-2651-4

Manufactured in China.

8 7 6 5 4 3 2 1

Microwave Cooking: Microwave ovens vary in wattage. Use the cooking times as guidelines and check for doneness before adding more time.

Contents

Recipes

Your environment, your lifestyle, and your eating habits all contribute to your overall health. In the end, it's the choices you make every day that add up to have the biggest impact. When you learn to make good choices, you and your family will enjoy the benefits for years to come.

The important thing is to be physically active and develop healthy eating habits. That means eating a wide variety of foods that promote good health.

MAKING GOOD FOOD CHOICES

Whether you are eating at home or dining out, follow the recommendations below to help protect your heart:

Eat a variety of nutritious foods from all the food groups.

- Eat a diet rich in vegetables and fruits.
- Choose whole-grain, high-fiber foods.
- Eat fish, preferably oily fish, at least twice a week.

Limit foods that are high in calories but low in nutrients.

- Limit how much saturated fat, trans fat, and cholesterol you eat.
- Choose fat-free and low-fat dairy products.
- Cut back on beverages and foods with added sugars.
- Choose and prepare foods with little or no salt.
- If you drink alcohol, drink in moderation.

Read nutrition facts labels and ingredients lists when you choose foods.

For more information on the updated American Heart Association Dietary and Lifestyle Recommendations, visit **americanheart.org**.

HOW TO USE THESE RECIPES

To help you with meal planning, each recipe includes a nutrition analysis. Use the analyses and the information below to determine how to best fit each dish into your overall eating plan.

- Each analysis is for a single serving; garnishes or optional ingredients are not included.

- When ingredient options are listed, the first one is analyzed. When a range of ingredients is given, the average is analyzed.

- Values for saturated, monounsaturated, and polyunsaturated fats are rounded and may not add up to the amount listed for total fat. Total fat also includes other fatty substances and glycerol.

- Processed foods can be very high in sodium. To keep levels of sodium in our recipes low, we use unprocessed foods or low-sodium products when possible, and we add table salt sparingly for flavor. This way you control the amount of salt you add. If you use the amounts specified, you will not raise the sodium level as much as if you used a food processed with salt.

- The low-fat cheese we use for analysis has no more than 6 grams of fat per ounce.

- Meat statistics are based on cooked lean meat with all visible fat removed.

- We use 90% fat-free ground beef for analysis.

- When analyzing recipes that call for alcohol, we estimate that most of the alcohol calories evaporate during cooking.

- We use the abbreviations "g" for gram and "mg" for milligram.

Sweet Potato Chips

Serves 4 ▪ *½ cup per serving*

12 **ounces sweet potatoes, peeled and cut into ⅛-inch-thick slices (about 2 cups)**
   Olive oil cooking spray
¼ **teaspoon salt**

Preheat the oven to 375°F. Place a wire cooling rack on a large baking sheet.

On a work surface, lightly spray both sides of the sweet potato slices with the cooking spray. Arrange the potato slices on the wire rack in a single layer (do not crowd).

Bake for 20 minutes. Remove from the oven. Sprinkle with the salt and toss gently. Serve immediately for peak flavor and texture. (Otherwise, the moisture in the potatoes will cause the chips to lose their crispness.)

Per Serving: Calories 92; Total Fat 0 g; Saturated Fat 0 g; Polyunsaturated Fat 0 g; Monounsaturated Fat 0 g; Cholesterol 0 mg; Sodium 175 mg; Carbohydrates 21 g; Total Sugars 5 g; Dietary Fiber 3 g; Protein 1 g

Dietary Exchanges: 1½ Starch

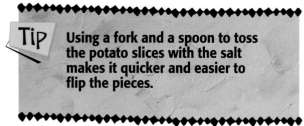

Tip **Using a fork and a spoon to toss the potato slices with the salt makes it quicker and easier to flip the pieces.**

Appetizers
& Snacks

Black-Eyed-Pea Hummus

Serves 12 ▪ *2 tablespoons per serving*

15-ounce can no-salt-added black-eyed peas, rinsed and drained
⅓ **cup fat-free or light sour cream**
¼ **cup water**
1 **medium green onion, cut into 2-inch pieces**
½ **teaspoon ground cumin**
1 **medium garlic clove**
½ **teaspoon salt**
¼ **teaspoon red hot-pepper sauce**

Put all the ingredients in a food processor or blender.
Process until smooth, stopping occasionally to scrape the
side with a rubber scraper. Serve at room temperature
or cover with plastic wrap and refrigerate for up to 48 hours.

Per Serving: Calories 38; Total Fat 0 g; Saturated Fat 0 g; Polyunsaturated Fat 0 g;
Monounsaturated Fat 0 g; Cholesterol 1 mg; Sodium 104 mg; Carbohydrates 7 g;
Total Sugars 2 g; Dietary Fiber 2 g; Protein 2 g

Dietary Exchanges: ½ Starch

Chicken Bites with Honey Mustard Dipping Sauce

Serves 10 ▪ *3 pieces chicken and 1 tablespoon sauce per serving*

Vegetable oil spray
1 cup fat-free or low-fat plain yogurt
1 pound chicken tenders, all visible fat discarded, cut into 30 pieces

Coating Mixture

½ cup yellow cornmeal
⅓ cup plain dry bread crumbs
2 tablespoons all-purpose flour
1 tablespoon plus 1 teaspoon shredded or grated Parmesan cheese
1 teaspoon paprika
½ teaspoon dried basil, crumbled
½ teaspoon garlic powder
¼ teaspoon salt

Honey–Mustard Sauce

½ cup fat-free or light sour cream
3 tablespoons Dijon mustard
2 tablespoons honey

Preheat the oven to 375°F. Lightly spray a large baking sheet with vegetable oil spray.

Put yogurt in a medium bowl. Add the chicken, stirring to coat. Set aside.

In another medium bowl, stir together the coating mixture ingredients.

Using tongs, dip a few pieces of chicken at a time in the coating mixture, turning gently to coat. Arrange the chicken in a single layer on the baking sheet. Lightly spray the chicken with vegetable oil spray.

Bake for 20 minutes, or until the chicken is no longer pink in the center and the coating is crisp.

Meanwhile, in a small bowl, whisk together the sauce ingredients.

To serve, arrange the chicken pieces on a platter with the sauce on the side.

Per Serving: Calories 143; Total Fat 1.5 g; Saturated Fat 0.5 g; Polyunsaturated Fat 0.5 g; Monounsaturated Fat 0.5 g; Cholesterol 29 mg; Sodium 247 mg; Carbohydrates 18 g; Total Sugars 7 g; Dietary Fiber 1 g; Protein 15 g

Dietary Exchanges: 1 Starch, 1½ Very Lean Meat

Creamy Corn Chowder

Serves 5 ▪ *1 cup per serving*

Vegetable oil spray
1 **tablespoon light tub margarine**
½ **cup chopped onion**
½ **cup diced celery**
1¼ **cups water**
1 **small baking potato, peeled and cut into ½-inch cubes (about 1 cup)**
14¾-ounce can no-salt-added cream-style corn, undrained
1½ **cups frozen whole-kernel corn, thawed**
1 **to 2 teaspoons sugar**
1 **teaspoon salt-free powdered chicken bouillon**
¼ **teaspoon salt**
⅛ **teaspoon white pepper**
1 **cup fat-free half-and-half**
1 **tablespoon all-purpose flour**
2 **tablespoons minced fresh parsley**

Lightly spray a medium saucepan with vegetable oil spray. Melt the margarine over medium heat. Add the onion and celery. Cook for 5 minutes, or until soft but not brown, stirring occasionally. Stir in the water, potato, both corns, sugar, bouillon, salt, and pepper. Increase the heat to medium high and bring to a boil. Reduce the heat and simmer, covered, for 20 minutes, or until the potatoes are just tender, stirring occasionally.

Pour the half-and-half into a small bowl and whisk in the flour. Stir into the soup. Stir in the parsley. Simmer for 15 minutes, or until the soup has thickened, stirring frequently.

Tip To further thicken the soup, simmer for another 10 to 15 minutes. To thin, stir in 1 to 2 tablespoons fat-free half-and-half or fat-free milk.

Per Serving: Calories 184; Total Fat 1.5 g; Saturated Fat 0 g; Polyunsaturated Fat 0.5 g; Monounsaturated Fat 0.5 g; Cholesterol 0 mg; Sodium 200 mg; Carbohydrates 41 g; Total Sugars 10 g; Dietary Fiber 3 g; Protein 7 g
Dietary Exchanges: 2½ Starch

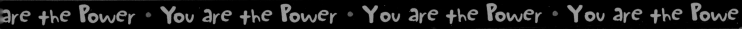
Soups

Old-Fashioned Vegetable-Barley Soup

Serves 4 ▪ *1¼ cups per serving*

Vegetable oil spray
- **1 teaspoon olive oil**
- **½ medium onion, chopped**
- **½ medium rib of celery, chopped**
- **1 medium garlic clove, minced**
- **14.5-ounce can no-salt-added diced tomatoes, undrained**
- **1½ cups frozen mixed vegetables**
- **1½ cups low-sodium vegetable broth**
- **1 cup chopped kale**
- **½ cup water**
- **¼ cup uncooked quick-cooking barley**
- **½ teaspoon dried basil, crumbled**
- **½ teaspoon dried oregano, crumbled**
- **⅛ teaspoon pepper**
- **1 tablespoon plus 1 teaspoon shredded or grated Parmesan cheese**

Lightly spray a large Dutch oven with vegetable oil spray. Add the oil and swirl to coat the bottom. Cook the onion and celery over medium-high heat until golden, about 3 minutes, stirring occasionally. Add the garlic and cook for 10 seconds. Stir in the remaining ingredients except the Parmesan. Bring to a boil over medium-high heat. Reduce the heat and simmer, covered, for 10 to 12 minutes, or until the barley is cooked.

To serve, ladle into soup bowls and sprinkle with the Parmesan.

Per Serving: Calories 129; Total Fat 2 g; Saturated Fat 0.5 g; Polyunsaturated Fat 0.5 g; Monounsaturated Fat 1 g; Cholesterol 1 mg; Sodium 78 mg; Carbohydrates 24 g; Total Sugars 5 g; Dietary Fiber 5 g; Protein 6 g

Dietary Exchanges: 1 Starch, 2 Vegetable

> **Tip** Look for bags of washed and chopped kale in the produce section of your supermarket.

Old-Fashioned Vegetable-Barley Soup with Dumplings

Serves 4 ▪ *1¼ cups soup and 1 dumpling per serving*

Prepare and cook the soup as directed on page 14, omitting the Parmesan. In a small bowl, combine ⅔ cup reduced-fat all-purpose baking mix (lowest sodium available) and 2 tablespoons finely chopped kale. Stir in ¼ cup fat-free milk until moistened.

Drop 4 mounds into the simmering soup. Simmer, covered, for an additional 15 minutes, or until a wooden toothpick or cake tester inserted into a dumpling comes out clean. (Do not remove the cover while simmering.) To serve, ladle the soup into soup bowls and top each serving with a dumpling.

Per Serving: Calories 204; Total Fat 3 g; Saturated Fat 0.5 g; Polyunsaturated Fat 0.5 g; Monounsaturated Fat 1 g; Cholesterol 0 mg; Sodium 290 mg; Carbohydrates 39 g; Total Sugars 7 g; Dietary Fiber 5 g; Protein 7 g

Dietary Exchanges: 2 Starch, 2 Vegetable

Green Bean Salad Vinaigrette

Serves 12 ▪ *½ cup per serving*

1	quart water for fresh green beans or ¼ cup for frozen
1	pound fresh or frozen green beans
1½	tablespoons raspberry vinegar or red or white wine vinegar
¾	to 1 teaspoon prepared mustard
½	teaspoon finely snipped fresh thyme leaves or 1½ teaspoons dried, crumbled
½	teaspoon finely snipped fresh parsley or 1½ teaspoons dried, crumbled
½	teaspoon honey
½	medium garlic clove, minced
¼	cup canola or corn oil
¼	teaspoon salt
⅛	teaspoon pepper, or to taste
1	medium red bell pepper, cut lengthwise into thin strips
½	to 1 small red onion, cut lengthwise into thin strips
¼	teaspoon fresh lemon zest

In a large saucepan, bring the water to a boil over high heat. Add the beans and boil for 5 minutes.

Meanwhile, fill a large bowl with cold water. When the beans are ready, drain them in a colander, then transfer to the cold water to stop the cooking process. Once the green beans are cold, drain well and pat dry.

While the beans are cooling, whisk together the vinegar, mustard, thyme, parsley, honey, and garlic in another large bowl. Slowly whisk in the oil, continuing to whisk until well combined. Whisk in the salt and pepper.

Add the green beans, bell pepper, and onion to the vinaigrette, tossing to coat. Cover and refrigerate for at least 30 minutes before serving. Just before serving, sprinkle with the lemon zest.

Per Serving: Calories 60; Total Fat 5 g; Saturated Fat 0.5 g; Polyunsaturated Fat 1.5 g; Monounsaturated Fat 3 g; Cholesterol 0 mg; Sodium 55 mg; Carbohydrates 4 g; Total Sugars 2 g; Dietary Fiber 2 g; Protein 1 g

Dietary Exchanges: 1 Vegetable

Salads

Sweet Country Coleslaw

Serves 4 ▪ *½ cup per serving*

2   **tablespoons fat-free or light sour cream**
1   **tablespoon plus 1 teaspoon sugar**
1   **tablespoon fat-free or light mayonnaise**
1   **teaspoon cider vinegar**
¼   **teaspoon celery seeds (optional)**
⅛   **teaspoon salt**
⅛   **teaspoon pepper**
4   **cups packaged shredded cabbage and carrot mix**

In a medium bowl, stir together all the ingredients except the cabbage and carrot mix. Stir in the cabbage and carrot mix until well coated. (The mixture will be very thick.) Let stand for 15 minutes before serving. (The coleslaw will shrink in volume by about half.)

Per Serving: Calories 44; Total Fat 0 g; Saturated Fat 0 g; Polyunsaturated Fat 0 g; Monounsaturated Fat 0 g; Cholesterol 2 mg; Sodium 126 mg; Carbohydrates 9 g; Total Sugars 7 g; Dietary Fiber 1 g; Protein 1 g

Dietary Exchanges: ½ Other Carbohydrate

Potato Salad

Serves 4 ▪ *½ cup per serving*

2	cups water
10	ounces red potatoes, peeled and cut into ½-inch cubes
½	medium rib of celery, finely chopped
⅓	cup finely chopped yellow or white onion (about 1 small) or green onions (about 3 medium, green and white parts)
2	tablespoons fat-free or light mayonnaise
2	tablespoons fat-free or light sour cream
2	to 3 teaspoons sweet pickle relish
½	teaspoon prepared mustard
¼	teaspoon salt
⅛	teaspoon pepper

In a medium saucepan, bring the water to a boil over high heat. Add the potatoes and return to a boil. Reduce the heat and simmer, covered, for 4 to 5 minutes, or until the potatoes are just tender. Drain in a colander. Run the potatoes under cold water for about 20 seconds to stop the cooking process. Drain well in a colander.

In a medium bowl, stir together the remaining ingredients. Using a rubber scraper, gently fold the potatoes into the mixture. Cover and refrigerate for 2 to 3 hours. The flavor and texture are at their peak if the salad is served the day it is made.

Per Serving: Calories 70; Total Fat 0.5 g; Saturated Fat 0 g; Polyunsaturated Fat 0 g; Monounsaturated Fat 0 g; Cholesterol 2 mg; Sodium 251 mg; Carbohydrates 14 g; Total Sugars 3 g; Dietary Fiber 2 g; Protein 2 g

Dietary Exchanges: 1 Starch

Ambrosia Fruit Salad

Serves 6 ▪ *½ cup per serving*

> | 15.25-ounce can pineapple chunks in their own juice
> | 11-ounce can mandarin oranges in water or light syrup
> 1 | medium apple, cut into bite-size pieces
> ½ | cup halved green or red grapes
> 1 | tablespoon honey
> ¼ | teaspoon ground cinnamon
> ¼ | cup plus 2 tablespoons low-fat granola with raisins

Drain the pineapple, reserving ⅓ cup juice. Drain the mandarin oranges.

In a medium bowl, stir together the pineapple, oranges, apple, and grapes.

In a small bowl, stir together the reserved pineapple juice, honey, and cinnamon. Pour over the fruit mixture, stirring gently to coat.

To serve, spoon the fruit into bowls. Sprinkle each serving with granola.

Per Serving: Calories 114; Total Fat 0.5 g; Saturated Fat 0 g; Polyunsaturated Fat 0 g; Monounsaturated Fat 0 g; Cholesterol 0 mg; Sodium 17 mg; Carbohydrates 29 g; Total Sugars 24 g; Dietary Fiber 2 g; Protein 1 g

Dietary Exchanges: ½ Starch, 1½ Fruit

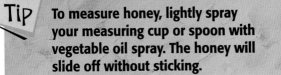

Tip To measure honey, lightly spray your measuring cup or spoon with vegetable oil spray. The honey will slide off without sticking.

Salmon Patties with Sour Cream and Dijon Topping

Serves 4 ▪ *1 salmon patty and 2 teaspoons topping per serving*

Salmon Patties

7.1-ounce vacuum-sealed pouch pink salmon
¼ **cup plain dry bread crumbs**
¼ **cup grated onion**
2 **tablespoons yellow cornmeal**
2 **tablespoons fat-free or light mayonnaise**
White of 1 large egg
1 **tablespoon snipped fresh parsley**
1 **teaspoon salt-free extra-spicy seasoning blend**
½ **teaspoon red hot-pepper sauce**

· · · · · · · · · · · · ·

2 **tablespoons all-purpose flour**
1 **tablespoon yellow cornmeal**
2 **teaspoons canola or corn oil**

Topping

2 **tablespoons fat-free or light sour cream**
1 **tablespoon Dijon mustard**
⅛ **teaspoon cayenne**

In a medium bowl, flake the salmon. Stir in the remaining salmon patty ingredients. Shape the mixture into 4 patties, each about ½ inch thick.

In a small bowl, combine the flour and 1 tablespoon cornmeal. Press the sides and edge of each salmon patty into the mixture (no need to shake off the excess).

Heat a large nonstick skillet over medium-high heat. Add the oil and swirl to coat the bottom. Heat the oil. Cook the patties for 5 minutes. Turn and cook for 5 to 7 minutes, or until golden brown.

Meanwhile, in a small bowl, stir together the topping ingredients. Spoon the topping over each patty.

Per Serving: Calories 166; Total Fat 5 g; Saturated Fat 1 g; Polyunsaturated Fat 1 g; Monounsaturated Fat 1.5 g; Cholesterol 20 mg; Sodium 463 mg; Carbohydrates 17 g; Total Sugars 2 g; Dietary Fiber 1 g; Protein 13 g

Dietary Exchanges: 1 Starch, 1½ Lean Meat

Seafood

Blackened Tilapia

Serves 4 ▪ *3 ounces fish per serving*

4 **tilapia fillets (about 4 ounces each)**
2 **teaspoons paprika**
1 **teaspoon dried oregano, crumbled**
1 **teaspoon chili powder**
¼ **teaspoon salt**
¼ **teaspoon pepper**
⅛ **teaspoon cayenne**
2 **teaspoons olive oil**
1 **medium lemon, quartered (optional)**

Rinse the fish and pat dry with paper towels.

In a small bowl, stir together the paprika, oregano, chili powder, salt, pepper, and cayenne. Sprinkle over both sides of the fish. Using your fingertips, gently press the mixture into the fish so it will adhere.

Heat a large nonstick skillet over medium-high heat. Add the oil and swirl to coat the bottom. Cook the fish for 2 minutes. Turn and cook for 2 to 3 minutes, or until the fish flakes easily when tested with a fork.

Serve with the lemon wedges.

Per Serving: Calories 136; Total Fat 4.5 g; Saturated Fat 1 g; Polyunsaturated Fat 1 g; Monounsaturated Fat 2 g; Cholesterol 57 mg; Sodium 205 mg; Carbohydrates 1 g; Total Sugars 0 g; Dietary Fiber 1 g; Protein 23 g

Dietary Exchanges: 3 Lean Meat

Cheddar and Tuna Noodles

Serves 5 ▪ *1½ cups per serving*

- 6 cups water
- 4 ounces dried no-yolk egg noodles
- 10 ounces frozen mixed vegetables
  - 10.75-ounce can low-fat, reduced-sodium condensed cream of mushroom soup
  - 4-ounce jar sliced pimientos, rinsed if desired and drained
- ¼ cup snipped fresh parsley
- ¼ cup fat-free half-and-half or fat-free milk
  - 3-ounce vacuum-sealed pouch light tuna
- 3 ounces (about ¾ cup) shredded fat-free or low-fat sharp Cheddar cheese

In a 12-inch nonstick skillet, bring the water to a boil over high heat. Stir in the noodles. Return to a boil. Reduce the heat and simmer, covered, for 4 minutes. Stir in the mixed vegetables. Cook, covered, for 4 minutes, or until the green beans are tender-crisp. Drain well in a colander. Return to the skillet.

In a small bowl, whisk together the soup, pimientos, parsley, and half-and-half. Spoon over the noodle mixture. Sprinkle with the tuna. Top with the Cheddar. Do not stir. Set the heat at low. Cook, covered, for 10 minutes to heat slightly and allow the Cheddar to melt.

Per Serving: Calories 215; Total Fat 3.5 g; Saturated Fat 1.5 g; Polyunsaturated Fat 0 g; Monounsaturated Fat 0.5 g; Cholesterol 18 mg; Sodium 459 mg; Carbohydrates 32 g; Total Sugars 5 g; Dietary Fiber 4 g; Protein 15 g

Dietary Exchanges: 2 Starch, 1½ Very Lean Meat

Shrimp Gumbo

Serves 6 ▪ 1 cup gumbo and ⅓ cup rice per serving

2	tablespoons all-purpose flour
2	teaspoons olive oil
1	medium onion, chopped
1	medium green bell pepper, chopped
1	to 1½ medium ribs of celery, sliced
	14.5-ounce can no-salt-added diced tomatoes, undrained
10	ounces frozen sliced okra, thawed (about 2 cups)
10½	ounces canned fat-free, low-sodium chicken broth
2	bay leaves
1	tablespoon Worcestershire sauce (lowest sodium available)
1	teaspoon sugar
¾	teaspoon dried thyme, crumbled
4	ounces canned fat-free, low-sodium chicken broth
1	pound fresh or frozen peeled raw medium shrimp, thawed if frozen
1	tablespoon olive oil
¾	teaspoon salt
¼	teaspoon red hot-pepper sauce
1	cup uncooked instant brown or white rice

Heat a Dutch oven over medium heat. Cook the flour for 1 to 1½ minutes, or until beginning to turn off-white, stirring constantly. Do not overcook. Transfer to a plate.

Add 2 teaspoons oil to the pot and swirl to coat the bottom. Cook the onion, bell pepper, and celery for 5 minutes, stirring frequently. Stir in the undrained tomatoes, okra, 10½ ounces broth, bay leaves, Worcestershire sauce, sugar, and thyme.

In a jar with a tight-fitting lid, combine the remaining broth and the reserved flour. Cover and shake until completely blended. Stir into the tomato mixture. Bring to a boil over high heat. Reduce the heat and simmer, covered, for 25 minutes, or until the okra is very tender and the mixture has thickened, stirring frequently.

Stir in the shrimp. Cook, covered, for 5 minutes, or until the shrimp turn pink. Remove from the heat.

Stir in 1 tablespoon oil, salt, and hot-pepper sauce. Let stand for at least 15 minutes. Discard the bay leaves.

Meanwhile, prepare the rice using the package directions, omitting the salt and margarine.

To serve, spoon the rice into soup bowls. Ladle the gumbo over the rice.

Per Serving: Calories 205; Total Fat 5 g; Saturated Fat 0.5 g; Polyunsaturated Fat 1 g; Monounsaturated Fat 3 g; Cholesterol 112 mg; Sodium 461 mg; Carbohydrates 24 g; Total Sugars 6 g; Dietary Fiber 4 g; Protein 16 g

Dietary Exchanges: 1 Starch, 2 Vegetable, 2 Lean Meat

Tip **The flavors will improve if the gumbo is refrigerated overnight.**

Oven–Fried Catfish with Tartar Sauce

Serves 4 ▪ *3 ounces fish and 1 tablespoon sauce per serving*

Vegetable oil spray
⅓ **cup yellow cornmeal**
2 **tablespoons all-purpose flour**
1 **teaspoon salt-free extra-spicy seasoning blend**
1 **teaspoon paprika**
½ **teaspoon onion powder**
½ **teaspoon garlic powder**
¼ **teaspoon salt**
¼ **teaspoon pepper**
¼ **cup fat-free or low-fat buttermilk**
1 **teaspoon fresh lemon juice**
4 **catfish fillets (about 4 ounces each)**
3 **tablespoons fat-free or light mayonnaise**
2 **tablespoons sweet pickle relish**
2 **teaspoons fresh lemon juice**
½ **teaspoon red hot-pepper sauce**
¼ **teaspoon sugar**
1 **medium lemon, quartered (optional)**

Preheat the oven to 450°F. Lightly spray a baking sheet with vegetable oil spray.

In a shallow bowl, stir together the cornmeal, flour, seasoning blend, paprika, onion powder, garlic powder, salt, and pepper.

In a large shallow bowl, stir together the buttermilk and 1 teaspoon lemon juice. Set the bowl beside the cornmeal mixture.

Rinse the fish and pat dry. Dip each fish fillet in the buttermilk mixture, turning to coat. Dredge in the cornmeal mixture, covering completely. Place on the baking sheet. Lightly spray the top of the fish with vegetable oil spray. Bake for 15 minutes, or until the fish is golden brown and flakes easily when tested with a fork.

In a small bowl, stir together the mayonnaise, relish, 2 teaspoons lemon juice, pepper sauce, and sugar. Spoon the sauce over the fish and garnish with the lemon.

Per Serving: Calories 194; Total Fat 4 g; Saturated Fat 1 g; Polyunsaturated Fat 1 g; Monounsaturated Fat 1 g; Cholesterol 68 mg; Sodium 367 mg; Carbohydrates 19 g; Total Sugars 4 g; Dietary Fiber 1 g; Protein 21 g

Dietary Exchanges: 1½ Starch, 3 Very Lean Meat

Sweet Spiced Salmon

Serves 4 ▪ *3 ounces fish per serving*

½	**tablespoon grated orange zest**
¼	**cup fresh orange juice**
2	**tablespoons fresh lemon juice**
4	**salmon fillets with skin (about 5 ounces each)**
1½	**tablespoons firmly packed dark brown sugar**
½	**teaspoon paprika**
½	**teaspoon curry powder**
½	**teaspoon salt**
¼	**teaspoon ground cinnamon**
⅛	**teaspoon cayenne**
	Vegetable oil spray
1	**medium lemon, quartered (optional)**

Set the orange zest aside in a small bowl.

In a large resealable plastic bag, combine the orange juice and lemon juice. Rinse the salmon and pat dry with paper towels. Add to the juice mixture. Seal the bag. Turn several times to coat evenly. Refrigerate for 30 minutes, turning occasionally.

Meanwhile, stir the brown sugar, paprika, curry powder, salt, cinnamon, and cayenne into the orange zest. Set aside.

Preheat the oven to 425°F. Line a baking sheet with aluminum foil. Lightly spray the foil with vegetable oil spray.

Remove the salmon from the marinade. Discard the marinade. Arrange the salmon with the skin side down on the baking sheet. Rub the brown sugar mixture over the salmon.

Bake for 14 minutes, or until the salmon flakes easily when tested with a fork.

To serve, use a metal spatula to lift the salmon flesh from the skin. Place the salmon on plates. Serve with the lemon wedges to squeeze over the salmon.

Per Serving: Calories 187; Total Fat 5 g; Saturated Fat 1 g; Polyunsaturated Fat 2 g; Monounsaturated Fat 1.5 g; Cholesterol 74 mg; Sodium 388 mg; Carbohydrates 6 g; Total Sugars 5 g; Dietary Fiber 0 g; Protein 28 g

Dietary Exchanges: ½ Other Carbohydrate, 4 Very Lean Meat

Tip **Marinate the salmon for only 30 minutes so the texture will remain firm.**

Spicy Oven-Fried Chicken

Serves 4 ▪ *3 ounces chicken per serving*

Vegetable oil spray
¼ **cup fat-free or low-fat buttermilk**
¼ **cup cornflake crumbs**
¼ **cup yellow cornmeal**
2 **tablespoons all-purpose flour**
1 **teaspoon salt-free extra-spicy seasoning blend**
1 **teaspoon garlic powder**
½ **teaspoon paprika**
¼ **teaspoon cayenne**
¼ **teaspoon salt**
⅛ **teaspoon dry mustard**
4 **boneless, skinless chicken breast halves (about 4 ounces each),
 all visible fat discarded**

Preheat the oven to 375°F. Lightly spray an 8- or 9-inch square baking pan or a baking sheet with vegetable oil spray.

Pour the buttermilk into a pie pan or shallow bowl.

In a large airtight plastic bag, combine the remaining ingredients except the chicken.

Set the pie pan, plastic bag, and baking pan in a row, assembly-line fashion. Put a piece of chicken in the buttermilk and turn to cover completely. Put the chicken in the plastic bag and shake to coat. Place the chicken in the baking pan. Repeat with the remaining chicken. Lightly spray the tops of the chicken with vegetable oil spray. Bake for 30 minutes, or until the chicken is no longer pink in the center and the coating is crisp.

Per Serving: Calories 195; Total Fat 1.5 g; Saturated Fat 0.5 g; Polyunsaturated Fat 0.5 g; Monounsaturated Fat 0.5 g; Cholesterol 66 mg; Sodium 264 mg; Carbohydrates 16 g; Total Sugars 1 g; Dietary Fiber 1 g; Protein 28 g

Dietary Exchanges: 1 Starch, 3 Very Lean Meat

Poultry

Red Beans and Rice

Serves 4 ▪ *1 cup bean mixture and ½ cup rice per serving*

1	teaspoon olive oil
6	ounces smoked turkey slices (lowest sodium available), chopped
1	teaspoon olive oil
1	large onion, chopped
1	medium green bell pepper, chopped
1	medium red bell pepper, chopped
1½	medium ribs of celery, finely chopped
2	medium garlic cloves, minced
	Vegetable oil spray
	15-ounce can no-salt-added red beans or kidney beans, rinsed and drained
	14.5-ounce can fat-free, low-sodium chicken broth
2	bay leaves
¼	teaspoon dried thyme, crumbled
⅛	teaspoon cayenne
1	to 2 teaspoons Worcestershire sauce (lowest sodium available)
⅛	teaspoon salt
1	cup uncooked instant brown or instant white rice

Heat a large nonstick skillet over medium-high heat. Add 1 teaspoon oil and swirl to coat the bottom. Cook the turkey for 1 to 2 minutes, or until beginning to brown on the edges, stirring constantly. Transfer to a plate, leaving as much oil as possible in the skillet.

Add the remaining 1 teaspoon oil to the skillet and swirl to coat the bottom. Add the onion, bell peppers, celery, and garlic. Lightly spray the vegetables with vegetable oil spray. Cook for 4 minutes, or until the onion is soft, stirring frequently. Stir in the beans, broth, bay leaves, thyme, and cayenne. Increase the heat to high and bring to a boil. Reduce the heat and simmer, covered, for 20 minutes, or until the onion, bell peppers, and celery are very tender, stirring occasionally. Using a fork, mash the mixture to thicken it slightly.

Stir in the turkey, Worcestershire sauce, and salt. Simmer for 10 minutes, stirring frequently. Remove from the heat. Let stand for 10 minutes to continue to thicken. Discard the bay leaves.

Meanwhile, prepare the rice using the package directions, omitting the salt and margarine.

To serve, spoon the rice onto a platter. Spoon the bean mixture on top.

Per Serving: Calories 276; Total Fat 5 g; Saturated Fat 1 g; Polyunsaturated Fat 0.5 g; Monounsaturated Fat 2 g; Cholesterol 23 mg; Sodium 539 mg; Carbohydrates 43 g; Total Sugars 8 g; Dietary Fiber 8 g; Protein 17 g

Dietary Exchanges: 2½ Starch, 1½ Vegetable, 1 Lean Meat

Sweet and Spicy Barbecue Chicken

Serves 4 ▪ *3 ounces chicken per serving*

4 skinless chicken breast halves with bone (about 6 ounces each), all visible fat discarded
¼ teaspoon garlic powder
⅛ teaspoon pepper

Sauce

⅓ cup no-salt-added ketchup
¼ cup firmly packed dark brown sugar
2 tablespoons cider vinegar
2 tablespoons honey
1 tablespoon Worcestershire sauce (lowest sodium available)
½ teaspoon salt
¼ teaspoon ground allspice
⅛ teaspoon cayenne (optional)

Preheat the broiler. Line the broiler pan with aluminum foil.

Sprinkle the chicken with the garlic powder and pepper. Broil the chicken about 4 inches from the heat for 12 minutes, or until slightly pink in the center, turning every 4 minutes. (The chicken will not be totally cooked at this point.)

Meanwhile, in a small saucepan, stir together the sauce ingredients. Bring to a boil over medium-high heat. Reduce the heat and simmer for 5 minutes, or until reduced to about ½ cup, stirring frequently. Remove from the heat. Put 2 tablespoons sauce in a small bowl, leaving the remaining sauce in the pan.

After 12 minutes, turn the chicken and brush with half the sauce in the pan. Broil for 2 minutes. Turn the chicken. Brush with the remaining sauce in the pan. Broil for 1 minute, or until the chicken is just beginning to brown and is no longer pink in the center.

To serve, put the chicken with the smooth side up on plates. Brush with the reserved 2 tablespoons sauce.

Per Serving: Calories 289; Total Fat 2 g; Saturated Fat 0.5 g; Polyunsaturated Fat 0.5 g; Monounsaturated Fat 0.5 g; Cholesterol 99 mg; Sodium 419 mg; Carbohydrates 27 g; Total Sugars 25 g; Dietary Fiber 0 g; Protein 39 g

Dietary Exchanges: 2 Other Carbohydrate, 5 Very Lean Meat

Baked Turkey Wings

Serves 4 ▪ *3 ounces turkey per serving*

- ½ **teaspoon garlic powder**
- ½ **teaspoon onion powder**
- ½ **teaspoon paprika**
- ½ **teaspoon salt**
- ¼ **teaspoon poultry seasoning**
- ¼ **teaspoon pepper**
- 1 **teaspoon olive oil**
- 2 **turkey wings with skin (about 3 pounds), all visible fat discarded**
- 4 **medium ribs of celery, quartered**

Preheat the oven to 350°F. Line a baking sheet with aluminum foil.

In a small bowl, stir together the garlic powder, onion powder, paprika, salt, poultry seasoning, and pepper.

Drizzle the oil over the turkey wings. Sprinkle with the garlic powder mixture.

Arrange the celery on the baking sheet so it will be a rack to keep the turkey from sitting in the grease. (It will also add flavor to the turkey.) Place the turkey on the celery.

Bake for 50 to 55 minutes, or until an instant-read thermometer reaches 165°F when inserted in the thickest part of the wing.

Discard the celery and the skin and all visible fat from the wings. Slice the turkey from the bone before serving.

Per Serving: Calories 185; Total Fat 4.5 g; Saturated Fat 1.5 g; Polyunsaturated Fat 1 g; Monounsaturated Fat 1.5 g; Cholesterol 104 mg; Sodium 403 mg; Carbohydrates 2 g; Total Sugars 1 g; Dietary Fiber 1 g; Protein 32 g

Dietary Exchanges: 4 Very Lean Meat

Chicken and Dumplings

Serves 4 ▪ 1½ cups and 7 dumplings per serving

1	chicken breast with bone, 1 chicken thigh, and 1 chicken leg (about 2½ pounds), skin and all visible fat discarded
4	cups water
2	cups fat-free, low-sodium chicken broth
⅛	teaspoon pepper
1	cup all-purpose flour
½	teaspoon salt-free all-purpose seasoning
¼	teaspoon baking soda
1½	tablespoons light tub margarine
⅓	cup fat-free or low-fat buttermilk (plus more as needed)
	All-purpose flour for dusting
1	large carrot, chopped
2	medium ribs of celery, chopped
½	medium onion, chopped
	Fresh parsley, finely snipped (optional)

In a large saucepan, combine the chicken, water, broth, and pepper. Bring to a simmer over medium-high heat. Reduce the heat and simmer, covered, for 45 to 50 minutes, or until the chicken is cooked through. Using a slotted spoon, transfer the chicken to a cutting board. Turn the heat off, leaving the pan of liquid on the burner. Let the chicken cool for 15 to 20 minutes, or until easy to handle. Remove from the bones. Cut the chicken into bite-size pieces.

Meanwhile, in a medium bowl, whisk together the 1 cup flour, all-purpose seasoning, and baking soda. Using a pastry blender or fork, cut in the margarine until the margarine pieces are about pea size. Stir in the buttermilk until the dough is just moistened. (Do not overmix or the dumplings will be tough.) If the mixture is too dry, add buttermilk, 1 tablespoon at a time, until the dough holds together.

Lightly sprinkle a flat work surface with the flour for dusting. Put the dough on the work surface. Knead lightly three or four times so the dough holds together in a ball and is very slightly elastic. With floured hands or a floured rolling pin, pat or roll the dough to ¼-inch thickness. With a knife or pizza cutter, cut the dough into 28 pieces, each about 2 inches long by 1 inch wide. Cover with a dry towel.

Return the chicken to the pan. Stir in the carrot, celery, and onion. Bring to a simmer over medium-high heat. Reduce the heat and simmer, covered, for 10 minutes, or until the vegetables are tender.

Stir in the dumplings. Reduce the heat and simmer, uncovered, stirring occasionally, for 6 to 8 minutes, or until the dumplings are cooked through and the cooking liquid has thickened. (Dumplings should be opaque in the center and not taste raw.) Garnish with parsley, if desired.

Per Serving: Calories 320; Total Fat 6 g; Saturated Fat 1 g; Polyunsaturated Fat 1.5 g; Monounsaturated Fat 2 g; Cholesterol 95 mg; Sodium 307 mg; Carbohydrates 29 g; Total Sugars 3 g; Dietary Fiber 2 g; Protein 35 g

Dietary Exchanges: 1½ Starch, 1 Vegetable, 4 Very Lean Meat

Tip

Time-Saver: Use 2 cups chopped cooked skinless chicken (cooked without salt) for the uncooked chicken, omit the water and pepper, and increase the broth to 6 cups. Add the vegetables as directed and continue with the rest of the recipe.

Chicken and Bayou Vegetables

Serves 4 ▪ *1 cup chicken mixture and ½ cup rice per serving*

Vegetable oil spray
12 **ounces boneless, skinless chicken breasts, all visible fat discarded, cut into ½-inch pieces**
1 **medium green bell pepper, chopped**
½ **large onion, chopped**
1 **medium rib of celery, thinly sliced**
   14.5-ounce can no-salt-added diced tomatoes, undrained
1 **cup fresh or frozen cut okra**
½ **cup water**
2 **medium bay leaves**
1 **teaspoon Cajun or Creole seasoning blend**
1 **teaspoon dried thyme, crumbled**
½ **teaspoon sugar**
¼ **cup snipped fresh parsley**
1 **tablespoon olive oil (extra-virgin preferred)**
¼ **teaspoon salt**
1 **cup uncooked instant brown rice**

Heat a Dutch oven over medium-high heat. Remove from the heat and lightly spray with vegetable oil spray (being careful not to spray near a gas flame). Cook the chicken for 2 minutes, or until beginning to lightly brown, stirring frequently. (The chicken will still be a bit pink in the center.) Transfer the chicken to a plate.

Put the bell pepper, onion, and celery in the Dutch oven. Lightly spray the vegetables with vegetable oil spray. Cook over medium-high heat for 4 minutes, or until the onion is soft, stirring frequently. Stir in the undrained tomatoes, okra, water, bay leaves, seasoning blend, thyme, and sugar. Bring to a boil over medium-high heat. Stir. Reduce the heat and simmer, covered, for 20 minutes, or until the celery is tender and the mixture is slightly thickened. Stir in the parsley, oil, salt, and chicken with any accumulated juices.

Remove from the heat and let stand, covered, for 15 minutes, or until the chicken is no longer pink in the center. Discard the bay leaves.

Meanwhile, prepare the rice using the package directions, omitting the salt and margarine.

To serve, spoon the rice into bowls. Ladle the chicken mixture over the rice.

Per Serving: Calories 260; Total Fat 5.5 g; Saturated Fat 1 g; Polyunsaturated Fat 1 g; Monounsaturated Fat 3 g; Cholesterol 49 mg; Sodium 348 mg; Carbohydrates 29 g; Total Sugars 6 g; Dietary Fiber 4 g; Protein 24 g

Dietary Exchanges: 1 Starch, 3 Vegetable, 2½ Lean Meat

Smothered Steak

Serves 4 ▪ 3 ounces steak and ½ cup vegetables per serving

2 **tablespoons all-purpose flour**
¼ **teaspoon pepper**
4 **eye-of-round steaks (about 4 ounces each), all visible fat discarded**
2 **teaspoons canola or corn oil**
8 **ounces sliced button mushrooms**
½ **medium onion, thinly sliced**
1 **cup fat-free, no-salt-added beef broth**
2 **tablespoons imitation bacon bits**
2 **teaspoons soy sauce (lowest sodium available)**
1 **teaspoon molasses**
1 **cup frozen green beans**

In a shallow bowl or plate, stir together the flour and pepper. Coat the steaks on both sides with the mixture, shaking off the excess.

Heat a large nonstick skillet over medium-high heat. Add the oil and swirl to coat the bottom. Cook the steaks for 2 to 3 minutes on each side, or until browned. Transfer to a plate.

In the same skillet, cook the mushrooms and onion for 2 to 3 minutes, or until the onion is tender-crisp, scraping to dislodge any browned bits and stirring occasionally. Stir in the broth, bacon bits, soy sauce, and molasses. Add the steaks. Bring to a simmer, still on medium high. Reduce the heat and simmer, covered, for 35 to 40 minutes, or until the steaks are almost tender. Stir in the green beans. Simmer for 6 to 8 minutes, or until the steaks are tender and the beans are cooked through.

Slow-Cooker Method: After browning the steaks and cooking the mushrooms and onion, put all the ingredients except the green beans in a slow cooker. Cook on low for 4 to 6 hours, adding the green beans for the last hour of cooking, or on high for 2 to 3 hours, adding the green beans for the last 30 minutes of cooking.

Per Serving: Calories 222; Total Fat 6.5 g; Saturated Fat 1.5 g; Polyunsaturated Fat 1 g; Monounsaturated Fat 3 g; Cholesterol 47 mg; Sodium 172 mg; Carbohydrates 11 g; Total Sugars 3 g; Dietary Fiber 2 g; Protein 30 g

Dietary Exchanges: ½ Starch, 1 Vegetable, 3 Lean Meat

Meats

Seared Pork and Roasted Vegetables

Serves 4 ▪ *3 ounces pork and 1 cup vegetables per serving*

> **Vegetable oil spray**
> 1 **pound medium red potatoes, quartered**
> 4 **medium carrots, cut crosswise into ½-inch slices**
> 1 **large onion, cut into ½-inch wedges**
> 2 **teaspoons olive oil**
> ½ **teaspoon dried thyme, crumbled**
> ¼ **teaspoon paprika**
> ¼ **teaspoon garlic powder**
> ¼ **teaspoon salt**
> ¼ **teaspoon pepper**
>   **1-pound pork tenderloin, all visible fat discarded**
> 2 **teaspoons olive oil**
> ¼ **teaspoon salt**

Preheat the oven to 425°F. Line a large baking sheet with aluminum foil. Lightly spray with vegetable oil spray.

Place the potatoes, carrots, and onion on the baking sheet. Drizzle with 2 teaspoons oil. Toss to coat.

Bake for 10 minutes. Stir the vegetables. Push the vegetables toward the edges of the baking sheet, keeping them in a single layer.

Meanwhile, in a small bowl, stir together the thyme, paprika, garlic powder, ¼ teaspoon salt, and pepper. Sprinkle over the pork.

Heat a medium nonstick skillet over medium-high heat. Add the remaining oil and swirl to coat the bottom. Cook the pork for 6 minutes, or until richly browned, turning every 2 minutes. Place the pork in the center of the baking sheet with the vegetables.

Bake for 15 minutes, or until the vegetables begin to brown and the internal temperature of the pork registers 155°F on an instant-read thermometer.

Transfer the pork to a cutting board (leave the vegetables on the baking sheet). Let the pork stand for 10 minutes so it will continue to cook. Slice the pork.

Meanwhile, continue cooking the vegetables for about 10 minutes, or until the potatoes are tender when pierced with a fork. Sprinkle with ¼ teaspoon salt. Toss to coat.

Serve the pork with the vegetables on the side.

Per Serving: Calories 253; Total Fat 8.5 g; Saturated Fat 2 g; Polyunsaturated Fat 1 g; Monounsaturated Fat 5 g; Cholesterol 63 mg; Sodium 395 mg; Carbohydrates 17 g; Total Sugars 8 g; Dietary Fiber 6 g; Protein 26 g

Dietary Exchanges: ½ Starch, 2 Vegetable, 3 Lean Meat

Honey-Glazed Meat Loaf

Serves 6 ▪ *3 ounces per serving*

Vegetable oil spray
¼ **cup fat-free milk**
Egg substitute equivalent to 1 egg, or 1 large egg
White of 1 large egg
1 **cup whole-wheat bread crumbs**
1 **pound lean ground beef (90 percent fat-free preferred) or ground turkey breast, ground without skin**
1 **cup canned no-salt-added diced tomatoes, drained**
½ **cup finely diced onion**
½ **cup finely diced green bell pepper (about ½ medium)**
¼ **cup no-salt-added tomato paste**
1 **medium garlic clove, minced**
½ **teaspoon salt**
½ **teaspoon dried thyme, crumbled**
½ **teaspoon dried oregano, crumbled**
¼ **teaspoon black pepper**
1 **pinch cayenne pepper**
½ **cup no-salt-added tomato paste**
1 **teaspoon dark brown sugar**
¼ **cup honey**

Preheat the oven to 350°F. Spray a 9×5×3-inch loaf pan with vegetable oil spray.

In a medium bowl, whisk together the milk, egg substitute, and egg white. Stir in the bread crumbs.

In a large bowl, stir together the beef, tomatoes, onion, bell pepper, ¼ cup tomato paste, garlic, salt, thyme, oregano, black pepper, and cayenne pepper. Stir in the milk mixture. Press into the loaf pan, smoothing the top. Bake for 45 minutes to 1 hour, or until the internal temperature registers 165°F on an instant-read thermometer.

In a small bowl, stir together ½ cup tomato paste, sugar, and honey until the sugar dissolves. Pour over the meat loaf. Let stand for 15 minutes before slicing.

Prepared with Beef—Per Serving: Calories 306; Total Fat 9 g; Saturated Fat 3 g; Polyunsaturated Fat 0.5 g; Monounsaturated Fat 3 g; Cholesterol 43 mg; Sodium 465 mg; Carbohydrates 37 g; Total Sugars 20 g; Dietary Fiber 4 g; Protein 21 g

Dietary Exchanges: 1 Starch, 2 Vegetable, 1 Other Carbohydrate, 2½ Lean Meat

Prepared with Turkey—Per Serving: Calories 257; Total Fat 2 g; Saturated Fat 0.5 g; Polyunsaturated Fat 0.5 g; Monounsaturated Fat 0.5 g; Cholesterol 52 mg; Sodium 444 mg; Carbohydrates 37 g; Total Sugars 20 g; Dietary Fiber 4 g; Protein 25 g

Dietary Exchanges: 1 Starch, 2 Vegetable, 1 Other Carbohydrate, 2½ Very Lean Meat

Skillet Pork with Cornbread Stuffing

Serves 4 ▪ *1 pork chop and ⅓ cup stuffing per serving*

- ¼ **teaspoon paprika**
- ¼ **teaspoon salt**
- ⅛ **teaspoon pepper**
- 4 **boneless, center-cut pork loin chops (about 4 ounces each), all visible fat discarded**
- 2 **teaspoons olive oil**
- 1 **cup fat-free, low-sodium chicken broth**
- 1 **medium onion, finely chopped**
- ⅓ **cup finely chopped celery**
- 1½ **tablespoons light tub margarine**
- 1½ **cups dry cornbread stuffing mix**
- ⅛ **teaspoon poultry seasoning**

Preheat the oven to 350°F.

In a small bowl, stir together the paprika, salt, and pepper. Sprinkle over one side of the pork. Heat a medium nonstick skillet over medium heat. Add the oil and swirl to coat the bottom. Cook the pork with the seasoned side down for 2 minutes, or until just beginning to lightly brown. Transfer with the browned side up to a plate.

Increase the heat to medium-high. Stir the broth, onion, and celery into the skillet, scraping to dislodge any browned bits. Bring to a boil. Reduce the heat and simmer, covered, for 6 minutes, or until the celery is tender. Remove from the heat.

Stir in the margarine. Gently stir in the stuffing and poultry seasoning to blend thoroughly. Spread evenly in the skillet. Add the pork with the browned side up, pressing slightly into the stuffing.

Bake, covered, for 25 minutes, or until the pork is barely pink in the center. Remove from the heat. Let stand for 5 minutes to let the pork finish cooking.

Per Serving: Calories 295; Total Fat 11 g; Saturated Fat 2.5 g; Polyunsaturated Fat 1 g; Monounsaturated Fat 5.5 g; Cholesterol 67 mg; Sodium 635 mg; Carbohydrates 20 g; Total Sugars 5 g; Dietary Fiber 2 g; Protein 27 g

Dietary Exchanges: 1 Starch, 1 Vegetable, 3 Lean Meat

Tip Covering the skillet during baking helps trap the juices being released from the pork and vegetables, moistening the dressing.

Vegetarian Two-Bean Chili

Serves 4 ▪ *1½ cups per serving*

Vegetable oil spray
1 **teaspoon olive oil**
1 **large onion, chopped**
2 **medium garlic cloves, minced**
14.5-ounce can no-salt-added stewed tomatoes with onions, celery, and bell peppers, undrained
½ **6-ounce can no-salt-added tomato paste**
15-ounce can no-salt-added black beans, undrained
15-ounce can no-salt-added dark red kidney beans, undrained
2 **tablespoons Worcestershire sauce (lowest sodium available)**
1 **tablespoon chili powder**
1 **tablespoon salt-free extra-spicy seasoning blend**
2 **teaspoons sugar**

Lightly spray a Dutch oven with vegetable oil spray. Add the oil and swirl to coat the bottom. Add the onion and cook over medium-high heat until golden, about 3 minutes, stirring frequently. Add the garlic and cook for 10 seconds. Add the undrained tomatoes, breaking up any large pieces with a spoon. Stir in the tomato paste. Stir in the remaining ingredients. Bring to a boil, still over medium-high heat, then reduce the heat and simmer for 15 minutes, stirring occasionally.

Per Serving: Calories 266; Total Fat 1.5 g; Saturated Fat 0 g; Polyunsaturated Fat 0.5 g; Monounsaturated Fat 1 g; Cholesterol 0 mg; Sodium 48 mg; Carbohydrates 51 g; Total Sugars 16 g; Dietary Fiber 12 g; Protein 15 g

Dietary Exchanges: 3 Starch, 1 Vegetable, ½ Very Lean Meat

Vegetarian
Entrées

Spaghetti and Vegetable Casserole

Serves 4 ▪ *1 cup vegetable mixture and ½ cup pasta per serving*

6	**ounces dried whole-wheat spaghetti**
2	**teaspoons olive oil**
½	**medium green bell pepper, cut into 1-inch pieces**
2	**medium garlic cloves, minced**
½	**medium eggplant (about 8 ounces), diced**
1	**small yellow summer squash (about 4 ounces), diced**
1	**small zucchini squash (about 4 ounces), diced**
	14.5-ounce can no-salt-added diced tomatoes, undrained
	8-ounce can no-salt-added tomato sauce
1	**teaspoon dried oregano, crumbled**
¼	**teaspoon salt**
¼	**teaspoon crushed red pepper flakes**
2	**medium green onions, thinly sliced**
	Vegetable oil spray
1	**cup (about 4 ounces) shredded part-skim mozzarella cheese**
¼	**cup (about 1 ounce) shredded or grated Parmesan cheese**

Prepare the spaghetti using the package directions, omitting the salt and oil. Drain well in a colander. Set aside.

Meanwhile, heat a medium saucepan over medium heat. Add the oil and swirl to coat the bottom. Cook the bell pepper and garlic for 2 to 4 minutes, or until the bell pepper is tender-crisp, stirring occasionally. Stir in the eggplant, yellow summer squash, and zucchini. Cook for 4 to 8 minutes, or until the vegetables are almost tender, stirring occasionally. (Add water, 1 tablespoon at a time, if the vegetables start to stick to the pan.) Stir in the undrained tomatoes, tomato sauce, oregano, salt, and red pepper flakes. Increase the heat to medium-high and bring to a boil. Reduce the heat and simmer for about 10 minutes, or until the flavors have blended. Stir in the green onions.

Meanwhile, preheat the oven to 350°F. Lightly spray an 8-inch square baking pan with vegetable oil spray.

Spoon half the spaghetti into the baking pan. Spoon half the vegetable mixture over the spaghetti. Sprinkle with half the mozzarella and half the Parmesan. Repeat.

Bake for 20 to 25 minutes, or until the cheeses are melted and the casserole is heated through.

Time-Saver: Instead of making this into a casserole, spoon ½-cup portions of the spaghetti onto plates and top with 1-cup portions of the vegetable mixture. Sprinkle with cheeses.

Per Serving: Calories 336; Total Fat 9 g; Saturated Fat 4 g; Polyunsaturated Fat 1 g; Monounsaturated Fat 3.5 g; Cholesterol 22 mg; Sodium 433 mg; Carbohydrates 49 g; Total Sugars 10 g; Dietary Fiber 11 g; Protein 18 g

Dietary Exchanges: 2 Starch, 4 Vegetable, 1 Lean Meat, 1 Fat

Peas with Snaps

Serves 6 ▪ *½ cup per serving*

14.5-ounce can fat-free, low-sodium chicken broth
12 **ounces (2½ cups) frozen black-eyed peas (cowpeas)**
  and 4 ounces (½ cup) frozen cut green beans or
  16 ounces (3 cups) frozen field peas and snaps
 ½ **teaspoon dried thyme, crumbled**
 ¼ **cup finely chopped green onions (about 2 medium)**
 2 **teaspoons olive oil (extra-virgin preferred)**
 ½ **teaspoon salt**

In a medium saucepan, bring the broth to a boil over high heat. Stir in the peas, beans, and thyme. Return to a boil. Reduce the heat and simmer, covered, for 22 minutes, or until the peas and beans are tender. Remove from the heat.

Stir in the green onions, oil, and salt. Cover and let stand for 10 minutes so the peas and beans absorb the flavors of the other ingredients. The standing time is very important in this recipe.

Per Serving: Calories 103; Total Fat 2 g; Saturated Fat 0.5 g; Polyunsaturated Fat 0.5 g; Monounsaturated Fat 1 g; Cholesterol 0 mg; Sodium 235 mg; Carbohydrates 16 g; Total Sugars 1 g; Dietary Fiber 4 g; Protein 6 g

Dietary Exchanges: ½ Very Lean Meat, 1 Starch

Vegetables
& Sides

Oven–Fried Green Tomatoes

Serves 4 ▪ *2 tomato slices per serving*

Vegetable oil spray
2 **large green tomatoes, about 2 inches high (about 1 pound)**
1 **tablespoon olive oil**
½ **cup yellow cornmeal (stone-ground preferred)**
  Paprika, to taste
¼ **teaspoon salt**

Preheat the oven to 425°F. Line a baking sheet with aluminum foil and lightly spray with vegetable oil spray.

Cut and discard a thin slice from the top and bottom of each tomato. Cut each tomato into 4 slices, each about ½ inch thick.

Pour the oil into a shallow bowl or plate. Put the cornmeal in another shallow bowl or plate. Set the two bowls and the baking sheet in a row, assembly-line fashion.

Lightly coat a tomato slice with the oil, then with the cornmeal, shaking off any excess. Place the tomato slice on the baking sheet. Repeat with the remaining tomato slices. Sprinkle lightly with paprika and half the salt. Using the prongs of a fork, gently turn the slices and repeat.

Bake for 10 minutes. Turn the slices. Bake for 8 minutes, or until tender. Remove from the oven. Turn the slices. Let stand for 3 to 4 minutes so the tomatoes will soften slightly.

Per Serving: Calories 112; Total Fat 4 g; Saturated Fat 0.5 g; Polyunsaturated Fat 0.5 g; Monounsaturated Fat 2.5 g; Cholesterol 0 mg; Sodium 158 mg; Carbohydrates 19 g; Total Sugars 4 g; Dietary Fiber 2 g; Protein 3 g

Dietary Exchanges: 1 Starch, 1 Vegetable, ½ Fat

Tip

Be sure to use the prongs of a fork to turn the tomatoes because a spatula may scrape off the coating.

Stone-ground cornmeal is preferred in this recipe because it provides a better texture.

Candied Sweet Potatoes

Serves 6 ▪ *½ cup per serving*

Vegetable oil spray
2 **medium sweet potatoes (about 2 pounds total), quartered**
  8-ounce can crushed pineapple in its own juice, undrained
½ **cup fresh orange juice**
¼ **cup firmly packed light brown sugar**
1 **tablespoon cornstarch**
1 **tablespoon light tub margarine**

Topping

2 **tablespoons firmly packed light brown sugar**
1 **tablespoon light tub margarine, melted**
¼ **cup all-purpose flour**
¼ **cup chopped pecans**
¼ **teaspoon ground cinnamon**

Lightly spray a 1½-quart shallow baking dish with vegetable oil spray.

Put the sweet potatoes in a large saucepan. Add water to cover. Bring to a boil over high heat and boil for 25 to 30 minutes, or until tender. Remove from the pan and let cool for 5 minutes. Discard the skins. Cut the potatoes into ¼-inch-thick slices. Place in the baking dish.

Meanwhile, in a small saucepan, stir together the pineapple, orange juice, ¼ cup brown sugar, cornstarch, and 1 tablespoon margarine. Cook over medium heat for 6 to 8 minutes, or until the mixture comes to a boil and thickens, stirring frequently. Reduce the heat and simmer for 5 minutes, stirring occasionally.

Preheat the oven to 350°F.

In a small bowl, combine the topping ingredients. Spoon the pineapple mixture over the sweet potatoes. Sprinkle with the topping. Bake for 30 to 35 minutes, or until heated through.

Per Serving: Calories 318; Total Fat 5 g; Saturated Fat 0.5 g; Polyunsaturated Fat 1.5 g; Monounsaturated Fat 3 g; Cholesterol 0 mg; Sodium 91 mg; Carbohydrates 64 g; Total Sugars 28 g; Dietary Fiber 6 g; Protein 4 g

Dietary Exchanges: 4 Starch, ½ Fruit

Tip **You can serve this side dish with the topping, as above; replace the topping with 1 cup miniature marshmallows sprinkled over the potatoes for the last 5 minutes of baking; or omit both the topping and the marshmallows.**

Collard Greens with Smoked Sausage

Serves 8 ▪ *½ cup per serving*

1 **teaspoon olive oil**
4 **ounces low-fat smoked turkey sausage, cut into ¼-inch cubes**
1 **teaspoon olive oil**
1 **medium onion, finely chopped**
14.5-ounce can fat-free, low-sodium chicken broth
1 **pound frozen chopped collard greens**
1½ **teaspoons sugar**
¼ **teaspoon salt**

Heat a large saucepan over medium heat. Add 1 teaspoon oil and swirl to coat the bottom. Cook the sausage for 2 to 3 minutes, or until the edges begin to richly brown, stirring frequently. Transfer to a plate; do not drain the pan.

Add 1 teaspoon oil to the pan. Cook the onion for 3 minutes, or until soft, stirring frequently. Stir in the broth. Increase the heat to high and bring to a boil. Stir in the collard greens. Return to a boil. Reduce the heat and simmer, covered, for 25 minutes, or until the greens are tender. Remove from the heat.

Stir in the sausage, sugar, and salt. Let stand, covered, for 10 minutes.

Per Serving: Calories 55; Total Fat 1.5 g; Saturated Fat 0.5 g; Polyunsaturated Fat 0 g; Monounsaturated Fat 1.5 g; Cholesterol 5 mg; Sodium 263 mg; Carbohydrates 7 g; Total Sugars 3 g; Dietary Fiber 2 g; Protein 4 g

Dietary Exchanges: 1½ Vegetable, ½ Lean Meat

Tip Adding sugar does not sweeten these greens; it removes some of the bitterness, mellowing the flavor.

Okra and Tomatoes

Serves 6 ▪ *½ cup per serving*

2	teaspoons olive oil
½	medium onion, chopped
½	medium green bell pepper, chopped
½	medium rib of celery, chopped
	14.5-ounce can no-salt-added tomatoes, undrained
10	ounces fresh okra, cut into ½-inch slices, or frozen sliced okra, thawed
½	teaspoon sugar
¼	teaspoon dried thyme, crumbled
½	teaspoon salt, divided use

Heat a large saucepan over medium-high heat. Add the oil and swirl to coat the bottom. Cook the onion, bell pepper, and celery for 4 minutes, or until the onion is soft, stirring frequently. Stir in the remaining ingredients except ¼ teaspoon salt. Bring to a boil. Reduce the heat and simmer, covered, for 15 minutes, or until the okra is very tender, stirring occasionally. Remove from the heat.

Stir in ¼ teaspoon salt. Let stand, covered, for 5 minutes.

Per Serving: Calories 50; Total Fat 1.5 g; Saturated Fat 0 g; Polyunsaturated Fat 0 g; Monounsaturated Fat 1 g; Cholesterol 0 mg; Sodium 208 mg; Carbohydrates 8 g; Total Sugars 4 g; Dietary Fiber 3 g; Protein 2 g

Dietary Exchanges: 1½ Vegetable, ½ Fat

Rich and Creamy Mac and Cheese

Serves 4 ▪ *½ cup per serving*

4 ounces dried elbow macaroni
4 slices low-fat American cheese, about ¾ ounce each
⅓ cup fat-free milk
2 tablespoons light tub margarine
1 teaspoon prepared mustard
½ teaspoon Worcestershire sauce (lowest sodium available)
⅛ teaspoon salt
⅛ teaspoon red hot-pepper sauce

In a large saucepan, prepare the macaroni using the package directions, omitting the salt and oil. Drain well in a colander. Return to the pan.

Add the remaining ingredients, stirring until the cheese melts. Cook over medium heat for 8 to 10 minutes, or until slightly thickened, stirring frequently. Remove from the heat. Let stand for 5 minutes to continue to thicken.

Per Serving: Calories 173; Total Fat 3.5 g; Saturated Fat 0.5 g; Polyunsaturated Fat 0.5 g; Monounsaturated Fat 1.5 g; Cholesterol 5 mg; Sodium 344 mg; Carbohydrates 24 g; Total Sugars 3 g; Dietary Fiber 1 g; Protein 9 g

Dietary Exchanges: 1½ Starch, 1 Lean Meat

Fiery Smothered Cabbage

Serves 4 ▪ *½ cup per serving*

1 small Napa cabbage
1 tablespoon olive oil
1 cup coarsely chopped onion
1 ounce extra-lean ham (lowest sodium available) or
   2 ounces smoked turkey breast (lowest sodium available),
   cut into bite-size cubes
1 cup fat-free, low-sodium chicken broth
1 ounce dry white wine (regular or nonalcoholic)
½ to 1 teaspoon black pepper
1½ teaspoons salt-free herb seasoning blend, such as garlic-herb
1 teaspoon crushed red pepper flakes
¼ teaspoon onion powder
¼ teaspoon garlic powder
¼ teaspoon salt
1 small red bell pepper, cut lengthwise into thin strips

Discard the outer leaves of the cabbage. Cut the remaining cabbage into quarters. Cut out and discard the core from each portion. Cut enough of the remaining leaves in long, fine shreds to measure 2 cups; do not chop.

Pour the oil into a large skillet and swirl to coat the bottom. Heat over medium heat. Cook the onion for about 2 minutes, or until it begins to soften, stirring frequently. Stir in the ham. Cook for about 1 minute, continuing to stir. Add the cabbage. Stir to combine. Stir in the broth, white wine, and black pepper. Bring to a simmer and cook for 5 minutes, or until the cabbage just begins to soften. Stir in the remaining ingredients except the bell pepper strips. Place the strips on the cabbage mixture. Reduce the heat and simmer, covered, for about 5 minutes, or until the strips have slightly softened.

Prepared with Ham—Per Serving: Calories 77; Total Fat 3.5 g; Saturated Fat 0.5 g; Polyunsaturated Fat 0.5 g; Monounsaturated Fat 2.5 g; Cholesterol 3 mg; Sodium 227 mg; Carbohydrates 7 g; Total Sugars 3 g; Dietary Fiber 2 g; Protein 3 g

Dietary Exchanges: 1½ Vegetable, 1 Fat

Prepared with Turkey—Per Serving: Calories 84; Total Fat 4 g; Saturated Fat 0.5 g; Polyunsaturated Fat 0.5 g; Monounsaturated Fat 2.5 g; Cholesterol 8 mg; Sodium 290 mg; Carbohydrates 8 g; Total Sugars 4 g; Dietary Fiber 2 g; Protein 4 g

Dietary Exchanges: 1½ Vegetable, 1 Fat

Smashed Red Potatoes

Serves 5 ▪ *½ cup per serving*

1 pound small red potatoes (about 7), quartered
¾ to 1 cup fat-free or low-fat buttermilk
3 tablespoons finely chopped green onions
(green part only)
1 tablespoon plus 1 teaspoon shredded or grated
Parmesan cheese
¼ teaspoon salt
⅛ teaspoon pepper

Put the potatoes in a medium saucepan. Pour in enough water to cover. Bring to a boil over high heat. Reduce the heat and simmer for 10 to 15 minutes, or until fork-tender. Drain thoroughly in a colander. Return to the saucepan.

Meanwhile, in a small saucepan, heat the buttermilk over medium-low heat for 5 to 7 minutes, or until hot, making sure it doesn't boil. Remove from the heat.

Using a potato masher, mash the potatoes, adding enough buttermilk to make them creamy. Add the remaining ingredients, stirring just until blended.

Per Serving: Calories 83; Total Fat 0.5 g; Saturated Fat 0 g; Polyunsaturated Fat 0 g; Monounsaturated Fat 0 g; Cholesterol 1 mg; Sodium 157 mg; Carbohydrates 19 g; Total Sugars 4 g; Dietary Fiber 2 g; Protein 4 g

Dietary Exchanges: 1 Starch

Tip

Overbeating mashed potatoes may cause them to become gummy. The best way to avoid this is to use a potato masher rather than a food processor or electric mixer. You can also achieve good results with a food mill, but it removes the nutritious potato skins. The amount of liquid needed (buttermilk in this recipe) depends on how hot and well drained the potatoes are when mashed and how warm the liquid is.

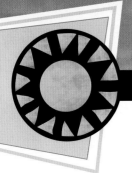
Sweet Potato Pancakes

Serves 4 ▪ *2 pancakes, 2 teaspoons margarine,
and 2 teaspoons syrup per serving*

1   **cup low-fat all-purpose baking mix (lowest sodium available)**
½   **15-ounce can sweet potatoes in light syrup, drained,
mashed with a fork until smooth**
⅔   **cup fat-free milk**
2   **tablespoons sugar**
½   **teaspoon ground cinnamon (optional)**
½   **teaspoon vanilla extract**
2   **teaspoons canola or corn oil, divided use**
2   **tablespoons plus 2 teaspoons light tub margarine**
2   **tablespoons plus 2 teaspoons maple syrup or sugar-free
pancake syrup**

In a medium bowl, stir together the baking mix, sweet potatoes,
milk, sugar, cinnamon, and vanilla until just blended. (Do not
overmix or the pancakes will be tough.)

Heat a large nonstick skillet over medium heat. Add 1 teaspoon
of the oil. Using a paper towel, spread the oil to leave a fine film
over the bottom of the skillet. Pour in a scant ¼ cup batter for
each of four pancakes. Cook for 2 minutes, or until puffy (bubbles
will not break the surface as in most pancake recipes). Lightly
spray a flat spatula with vegetable oil spray. Flip the pancakes.
Cook for 1 minute, or until golden on the bottom. Transfer to
a plate. Repeat with the remaining oil and remaining batter.

To serve, spread the margarine on the pancakes. Drizzle with
the syrup.

Per Serving: Calories 252; Total Fat 5 g; Saturated Fat 0 g; Polyunsaturated Fat 1 g;
Monounsaturated Fat 3 g; Cholesterol 1 mg; Sodium 417 mg; Carbohydrates 48 g;
Total Sugars 21 g; Dietary Fiber 2 g; Protein 4 g

Dietary Exchanges: 2 Starch, 1 Other Carbohydrate, ½ Fat

Breads
& Breakfasts

Southern Cornbread

Serves 9 ▪ *1 piece per serving*

Vegetable oil spray
 1 cup yellow cornmeal
 ½ cup all-purpose flour
 ½ cup whole-wheat flour
 2 tablespoons sugar
 ½ teaspoon baking soda
 ½ teaspoon baking powder
 ½ teaspoon salt
 1 cup no-salt-added cream-style corn, undrained
 ½ cup frozen whole-kernel corn, thawed
 ½ cup fat-free or low-fat buttermilk
 ¼ cup fat-free milk
 Egg substitute equivalent to 1 egg
 2 tablespoons canola or corn oil

Preheat the oven to 425°F. Lightly spray a 9-inch square or round baking pan or pie pan with vegetable oil spray.

In a large bowl, stir together the cornmeal, both flours, sugar, baking soda, baking powder, and salt. Make a well in the center.

In a medium bowl, stir together the remaining ingredients. Pour into the well in the flour mixture, stirring just until moistened. Spoon into the baking pan. Lightly spray the top of the batter with vegetable oil spray.

Bake for 20 to 25 minutes, or until a wooden toothpick or cake tester comes out clean when inserted in the center. Transfer the pan to a cooling rack and let cool for 5 to 10 minutes before slicing.

Per Serving: Calories 181; Total Fat 4 g; Saturated Fat 0.5 g; Polyunsaturated Fat 1 g; Monounsaturated Fat 2 g; Cholesterol 1 mg; Sodium 255 mg; Carbohydrates 34 g; Total Sugars 5 g; Dietary Fiber 3 g; Protein 5 g

Dietary Exchanges: 2½ Starch, ½ Fat

Angel Biscuits

Serves 26 ▪ *1 biscuit per serving*

¼	**cup lukewarm water (105°F to 115°F)**
	¼-ounce package active dry yeast
½	**teaspoon sugar**
2½	**cups all-purpose flour**
2	**tablespoons sugar**
½	**teaspoon baking powder**
½	**teaspoon baking soda**
⅓	**cup canola or corn oil**
1	**cup fat-free or low-fat buttermilk**
¼	**cup all-purpose flour, plus more as needed**
	Vegetable oil spray

In a medium bowl, stir together the water, yeast, and ½ teaspoon sugar until the yeast is dissolved. Let the mixture stand at room temperature for 5 minutes to activate the yeast (it should smell slightly fermented).

Meanwhile, in a large bowl, whisk together 2½ cups flour, 2 tablespoons sugar, baking powder, and baking soda. Using a pastry blender or fork, cut in the oil until the mixture is crumbly, with pieces about pea size.

In a small saucepan, heat the buttermilk over medium-low heat for 1 to 2 minutes, or until it reaches 110°F on an instant-read thermometer. Or microwave the buttermilk in a microwaveable container on 100 percent power (high) for 10 to 15 seconds, or until it reaches 110°F.

Stir the buttermilk into the yeast mixture. Then stir into the flour mixture until just moistened. The dough will be slightly sticky. (Do not overmix or the biscuits will be tough.) Cover and chill for 1 hour.

Sprinkle a flat work surface with about 2 tablespoons of the remaining flour. Put the dough on the floured surface. Sprinkle the dough with 2 tablespoons flour and knead three or four times. (If the dough is too sticky, add flour, 1 tablespoon at a time.) Shape into a flat disk. With floured hands or a floured rolling pin, pat or roll the dough to ½-inch thickness. Using a floured 2½-inch round cookie cutter or glass, cut out 26 biscuits.

Lightly spray a rimmed baking sheet with vegetable oil spray. Place the biscuits in a single layer on the baking sheet (the sides of the biscuits can touch). Cover the biscuits with a dry dish towel. Let rise in a warm, draft-free place for 1 hour, or until almost doubled in size.

Preheat the oven to 450°F. Bake for 10 to 12 minutes, or until the biscuits are golden brown and a wooden toothpick or cake tester inserted into the center comes out clean.

Per Serving: Calories 83; Total Fat 3 g; Saturated Fat 0.5 g; Polyunsaturated Fat 1 g; Monounsaturated Fat 2 g; Cholesterol 0 mg; Sodium 42 mg; Carbohydrates 12 g; Total Sugars 2 g; Dietary Fiber 0 g; Protein 2 g

Dietary Exchanges: 1 Starch, ½ Fat

Tip

To make the dough in advance, prepare as directed on page 66 through stirring the buttermilk-yeast mixture into the flour mixture. At this point, cover the bowl with a dish towel. Let rise at room temperature for 30 minutes to activate the yeast. Remove the towel. Cover the bowl tightly with plastic wrap and refrigerate for up to 3 days. When ready to make the biscuits, shape the dough and cut as directed above. Let rise for 1 to 1½ hours, or until almost doubled in size. Bake as directed above.

Creamy Cheese Grits

Serves 4 ▪ *½ cup per serving*

2¼ **cups water**
½ **cup quick-cooking grits**
2 **slices low-fat American cheese, about ¾ ounce each**
2 **tablespoons fat-free milk**
1 **tablespoon light tub margarine**
¼ **teaspoon salt**
½ **teaspoon Worcestershire sauce (lowest sodium available)**
⅛ **teaspoon garlic powder (optional)**
Pepper to taste (optional)

In a medium saucepan, bring the water to a rolling boil over high heat. Stir in the grits. Reduce the heat and simmer, covered, for 9 minutes, or until very thick, stirring occasionally. (This is a longer cooking time than directed on most packages because a thicker consistency is desired.) Remove from the heat.

Add the remaining ingredients except the pepper, stirring until the cheese has completely melted. Sprinkle with the pepper.

Per Serving: Calories 105; Total Fat 2 g; Saturated Fat 0.5 g; Polyunsaturated Fat 0.5 g; Monounsaturated Fat 0.5 g; Cholesterol 3 mg; Sodium 275 mg; Carbohydrates 17 g; Total Sugars 1 g; Dietary Fiber 0 g; Protein 5 g

Dietary Exchanges: 1 Starch, ½ Very Lean Meat

Baked Hush Puppies

Serves 24 ▪ *1 hush puppy per serving*

Vegetable oil spray
½ cup yellow cornmeal
½ cup all-purpose flour
½ cup frozen whole-kernel corn, thawed
¼ medium red bell pepper, finely chopped
1 teaspoon baking powder
½ teaspoon sugar
¼ teaspoon baking soda
¼ teaspoon salt
¼ teaspoon chili powder
⅓ cup fat-free or low-fat buttermilk
Egg substitute equivalent to 1 egg, or 1 large egg
1 tablespoon canola or corn oil

Preheat the oven to 425°F. Lightly spray two 12-cup mini muffin pans with vegetable oil spray.

In a medium bowl, stir together the cornmeal, flour, corn, bell pepper, baking powder, sugar, baking soda, salt, and chili powder. Make a well in the center.

Pour the buttermilk, egg substitute, and oil into the well. Stir until just moistened. (Do not overmix or the hush puppies will be tough.) Spoon the mixture into the muffin pans, filling each cup about two-thirds full.

Bake for 10 to 12 minutes, or until a wooden toothpick or cake tester inserted in the center comes out clean. Remove the hush puppies from the pan and transfer to a cooling rack. Let cool for at least 5 minutes before serving.

Per Serving: Calories 32; Total Fat 0.5 g; Saturated Fat 0 g; Polyunsaturated Fat 0 g; Monounsaturated Fat 0.5 g; Cholesterol 0 mg; Sodium 63 mg; Carbohydrates 6 g; Total Sugars 1 g; Dietary Fiber 0 g; Protein 1 g

Dietary Exchanges: ½ Starch

Tip A spring-loaded ice cream scoop makes easy work of filling muffin pans with batter. Available at most gourmet shops, the scoops come in a variety of sizes. Smaller ones can be used for mini muffins and cookie dough, and the larger sizes can be used for regular-size muffins.

Sweet Potato Cake with Zesty Orange Glaze

Serves 12 ▪ *3-inch square per serving*

Vegetable oil spray

Cake

18.5-ounce package spice cake mix
15-ounce can sweet potatoes in light syrup, drained
1¼ **cups water**
Egg substitute equivalent to 1 egg, or 1 large egg
Whites of 2 large eggs

Glaze

2 **teaspoons grated orange zest**
1 **cup fresh orange juice**
3 **tablespoons firmly packed dark brown sugar**
1½ **teaspoons cornstarch**

Preheat the oven to 350°F. Lightly spray a 13×9×2-inch baking pan with vegetable oil spray.

In a large mixing bowl, combine the cake ingredients. Using an electric mixer, beat according to the package directions. Pour the batter into the baking pan, smoothing the surface.

Bake for 30 minutes, or until a cake tester or wooden toothpick inserted in the center comes out almost clean. Transfer the pan to a cooling rack. Let the cake cool completely, about 1 hour.

Meanwhile, in a small saucepan, stir together the glaze ingredients until the cornstarch is dissolved. Bring to a boil over medium-high heat. Boil for 1 to 1½ minutes, or until thickened, stirring frequently. Remove from the heat. Let cool completely, about 20 minutes. Spoon over the cooled cake.

Per Serving: Calories 223; Total Fat 3 g; Saturated Fat 1.5 g; Polyunsaturated Fat 0 g; Monounsaturated Fat 1 g; Cholesterol 0 mg; Sodium 312 mg; Carbohydrates 47 g; Total Sugars 30 g; Dietary Fiber 0 g; Protein 2 g

Dietary Exchanges: 3 Other Carbohydrate, ½ Fat

Desserts

Cozy Peach Cobbler

Serves 9 ▪ *1 piece per serving*

Vegetable oil spray

Filling

¾	**cup peach nectar**
½	**cup fresh orange juice**
2	**tablespoons cornstarch**
1½	**teaspoons vanilla extract**
¼	**teaspoon ground cinnamon**
	29-ounce can sliced peaches, packed in juice, drained
1	**tablespoon firmly packed light brown sugar**

Topping

1	**tablespoon light tub margarine, melted**
1	**cup buttermilk pancake mix, whole-wheat preferred**
⅔	**cup all-purpose flour**
½	**cup sugar**
½	**teaspoon grated orange zest**
⅔	**cup fat-free evaporated milk**
2	**tablespoons firmly packed light brown sugar**
¼	**teaspoon ground cinnamon**

Preheat the oven to 400°F. Lightly spray an 8-inch square glass baking dish with vegetable oil spray.

In a medium saucepan, stir together the nectar, orange juice, cornstarch, vanilla, and cinnamon. Cook over medium heat for 6 to 8 minutes, or until the mixture comes to a boil and thickens, stirring frequently. Reduce the heat to medium low. Stir in the peaches and 1 tablespoon brown sugar. Reduce the heat and simmer for 5 minutes, stirring occasionally. Pour into the baking dish.

Meanwhile, in a medium bowl, stir together the margarine, pancake mix, flour, and sugar. Add the orange zest to the evaporated milk. Stir into the pancake mixture. Drop the dough by spoonfuls to form mounds on the warm fruit mixture.

In small bowl, combine the remaining brown sugar and cinnamon. Sprinkle over the cobbler.

Bake for 15 to 20 minutes, or until golden brown. Transfer the pan to a cooling rack and let cool for 10 minutes. Cut into squares. Serve warm or at room temperature.

Per Serving: Calories 226; Total Fat 1 g; Saturated Fat 0 g; Polyunsaturated Fat 0 g; Monounsaturated Fat 0.5 g; Cholesterol 1 mg; Sodium 154 mg; Carbohydrates 51 g; Total Sugars 30 g; Dietary Fiber 2 g; Protein 2 g

Dietary Exchanges: 1½ Starch, 1 Fruit, 1 Other Carbohydrate

> **Tip** If you don't find canned fruit nectars with the other fruit juices in the supermarket, look in the health food or Mexican food sections.

Coconut Layer Cake

Serves 12 ▪ *1 slice per serving*

       Vegetable oil spray
       18.5-ounce package white cake mix
1¼ **cups water**
       6-ounce jar baby food pureed pears
       Whites of 3 large eggs
 ½ **cup fat-free or light plain yogurt**
 ¼ **cup unsifted confectioners' sugar**
 2 **to 3 teaspoons grated lemon zest**
 2 **tablespoons fresh lemon juice**
 1 **or 2 drops yellow food coloring (optional)**
 8 **ounces (about 3 cups) frozen fat-free or light whipped topping,**
       thawed in refrigerator, divided
 3 **to 4 tablespoons sweetened flaked coconut**

Preheat the oven to 350°F. Lightly spray two 9-inch round cake pans with vegetable oil spray.

In a medium bowl, combine the cake mix, water, pears, and egg whites. Using an electric mixer, beat according to the package directions. Pour the batter into the cake pans, smoothing the tops.

Bake for 22 minutes, or until a cake tester or wooden toothpick inserted in the center comes out clean. Transfer the pans to cooling racks. Let cool for 10 minutes. Turn the cake onto the racks and let cool completely, about 1 hour.

Meanwhile, in a medium bowl, stir together the yogurt, confectioners' sugar, lemon zest, lemon juice, and food coloring. Fold in 1 cup of the whipped topping until completely blended. Cover and refrigerate until needed. Refrigerate the remaining whipped topping separately.

Place one cake layer on a large plate. Top with the yogurt mixture, then with the remaining cake layer. Spread the remaining whipped topping over the side and top of the cake. Sprinkle the top with the coconut. Refrigerate until ready to serve.

Tip It is important to thaw the whipped topping in the refrigerator, not at room temperature, so the filling and the frosting won't be runny.

Per Serving: Calories 249; Total Fat 4.5 g; Saturated Fat 2 g; Polyunsaturated Fat 0 g; Monounsaturated Fat 1 g; Cholesterol 0 mg; Sodium 331 mg; Carbohydrates 47 g; Total Sugars 27 g; Dietary Fiber 1 g; Protein 4 g

Dietary Exchanges: 3 Other Carbohydrate, 1 Fat

Bottom-Up Chess Pie

Serves 8 ▪ *1 slice per serving*

Vegetable oil spray
- 1 tablespoon corn oil stick margarine
- 16 low-fat graham crackers (4 full sheets), finely crushed
- 1⅓ cups sugar
- 2 tablespoons corn oil stick margarine, softened
- 2 large eggs
- ½ cup fat-free or low-fat buttermilk
  Whites of 2 large eggs
- 1 tablespoon white cornmeal or all-purpose flour
- 2 teaspoons vanilla extract
- ⅛ teaspoon salt

> **Tip**
> To soften margarine, place it in a small microwave-safe bowl and microwave on 100 percent power (high) for 8 to 10 seconds.

Preheat the oven to 375°F.

Lightly spray a 9-inch glass pie pan with vegetable oil spray. Put 1 tablespoon margarine in the pie pan. Microwave on 100 percent power (high) for 20 seconds, or until melted. Stir in the graham cracker crumbs until well blended. Press the mixture in the bottom of the pie pan.

Bake for 6 minutes, or until lightly golden. Transfer to a cooling rack and let cool slightly, about 15 minutes. Reduce the oven temperature to 350°F. Put an oven rack in the lowest position.

Meanwhile, in a medium mixing bowl, using an electric mixer on low speed, beat the sugar and 2 tablespoons margarine until well blended. Add the eggs. Beat well on medium speed until well blended. Add the remaining ingredients. Beat on high speed until well blended, about 30 seconds. Gently pour the mixture into the piecrust. (Some of the graham cracker mixture may float to the top.)

Bake for 40 to 45 minutes, or until a knife inserted in the center comes out clean. Transfer to a cooling rack and let cool for about 1 hour. The pie will continue to set as it cools, the crust will form a sweet and chewy topping, and the filling will settle to the bottom. Serve warm or chilled.

Per Serving: Calories 230; Total Fat 6 g; Saturated Fat 1 g; Polyunsaturated Fat 1 g; Monounsaturated Fat 3 g; Cholesterol 54 mg; Sodium 163 mg; Carbohydrates 41 g; Total Sugars 36 g; Dietary Fiber 0 g; Protein 4 g

Dietary Exchanges: 2½ Starch, 1 Fat

Banana Pudding

Serves 8 ▪ *½ cup per serving*

½ cup fat-free milk

¼ cup (2 ounces) light whipped cream cheese (in tub)

1-ounce package (4-serving size) fat-free, sugar-free instant reduced-calorie vanilla pudding mix

1½ cups fat-free milk

8 ounces (about 3 cups) frozen fat-free or light whipped topping, thawed in refrigerator

36 low-fat vanilla wafers

2 medium bananas, sliced

⅛ teaspoon ground nutmeg

1 medium banana

In a medium bowl, combine ½ cup milk, cream cheese, and pudding mix. Using an electric mixer on low speed, blend until smooth. With the mixer still on, gradually add 1½ cups milk, beating until smooth and scraping the side often. Fold in the whipped topping.

To assemble, line the bottom of a 2-quart bowl with 12 wafers in a single layer; some can go up the side if necessary. Top with 2 cups pudding mixture. Arrange half the banana slices over the pudding. Sprinkle with half the nutmeg. Repeat. Top with the remaining 12 wafers and pudding. Cover with plastic wrap and refrigerate overnight so the cookies will soften and achieve the proper texture.

To serve, slice the remaining banana. Arrange the slices on the pudding.

Per Serving: Calories 204; Total Fat 2.5 g; Saturated Fat 1 g; Polyunsaturated Fat 0 g; Monounsaturated Fat 0.5 g; Cholesterol 5 mg; Sodium 285 mg; Carbohydrates 39 g; Total Sugars 19 g; Dietary Fiber 1 g; Protein 4 g

Dietary Exchanges: 1½ Starch, 1 Fruit, ½ Fat

American Heart Association | **American Stroke Association**

POWER TO END STROKE℠
You are the Power

THE POWER IS IN YOUR HANDS

POWER TO END STROKE is a new education and awareness campaign that embraces and celebrates the culture, energy, creativity, and lifestyles of African Americans. The American Stroke Association, a division of the American Heart Association, has launched this campaign to make an impact on the incidence of stroke in our communities.

Cardiovascular disease, including stroke, causes more than a third of all deaths among African Americans. In a recent survey, the American Stroke Association found that although 70 percent of African American adults felt they were knowledgeable about stroke, only 30 percent knew how to define it correctly. Blacks are almost twice as likely as whites to have a stroke, yet only about 50 percent of the respondents knew the symptoms.

You can help change these numbers. Join the movement—*you* have the power to end stroke and win!

Put down the cigarettes and stop smoking.
Observe advice from your doctor and know your family's medical history.
Watch your weight and be physically active at least 30 minutes most days of the week.
Eat healthfully and avoid foods high in saturated fat, trans fat, cholesterol, and sodium.
Regulate and control high blood pressure, high blood cholesterol, and diabetes.

For more information on the American Stroke Association or how you can join the movement to fight stroke, call **1-888-4-STROKE** or visit **StrokeAssociation.org/power**.

YOLANDA KING JOINS THE FIGHT AGAINST STROKE

Daughter of the late Coretta Scott King and Dr. Martin Luther King, Jr., Yolanda King knows how important it is to pay attention to the risks for stroke and heart disease. She has teamed with the American Stroke Association to spread the word to the African American community as spokesperson for the **POWER TO END STROKE** program.

"Since my mother suffered a stroke, I know that it is doubly important for my family and me to pay special attention to the risk factors that we can control or eliminate," said Ms. King. African Americans are the racial/ethnic group that is most at risk for stroke. As part of her mission to encourage personal growth and positive social change, Ms. King wants African Americans to understand the health risks they face.

Please join Yolanda King in the fight against stroke by sharing awareness. "We want African Americans to first take the association's stroke pledge," Ms. King said. (Take the pledge on page 85.) "It's a promise for people to commit to not just 'survive,' but to 'thrive' by doing their part to make the right health choices for themselves, their families, and their communities to prevent and overcome stroke."

- Stroke and heart disease are not inevitable.
- You can take action to help prevent them.
- You are the Power.

American Heart Association. | American Stroke Association.

POWER TO END STROKE.SM

You are the Power

Stroke and heart disease are major health risks for Americans, especially for African Americans. But you have the power to take charge of your health by making good choices.

Good choices start with good information. Learn about the factors that increase your risk for cardiovascular disease and what you can do about them. Some factors—such as age and family history—can't be changed, but many can. **You have the power to affect these major risk factors: smoking, high blood pressure, high blood cholesterol, diabetes, obesity, and physical inactivity.** Get screened to find out if you're at risk. To start, go to page 87 to assess your risk. If you are at risk, work with your doctor to decide what actions you should take to reduce your risk.

DON'T SMOKE OR BREATHE TOBACCO SMOKE

Smoking or breathing tobacco smoke is the single greatest cause of preventable death among African Americans in the United States. Smoking greatly increases your risk of cardiovascular disease. The good news is that when you do stop smoking—no matter how long or how much you've smoked—your risk of heart disease and stroke drops rapidly. Within one to two years after you quit, your risk of coronary heart disease is substantially reduced.

If you don't smoke, don't start. If you do smoke, stop now! **You have the power to quit.** Ask your doctor to suggest a smoking cessation program that will work for you.

WATCH YOUR BLOOD PRESSURE

High blood pressure (hypertension) is often called the "silent killer" because it has no symptoms. It affects more than 40 percent of adult non-Hispanic blacks. Compared to whites, African Americans are more likely to have high blood pressure, develop it earlier in life, and have more severe cases.

Have your blood pressure checked at least once every two years or more often if you have a family history of high blood pressure, stroke, or heart attack. In between visits to your doctor, you can also check your blood pressure at your local drugstore. The first number (systolic pressure) measures the force of blood in your arteries when your heart beats. The second number (diastolic pressure) is the force while your heart rests between beats. Compare your results with the chart below to see if you're at risk. If your readings are in the prehypertension or high categories, work with your doctor to lower your blood pressure.

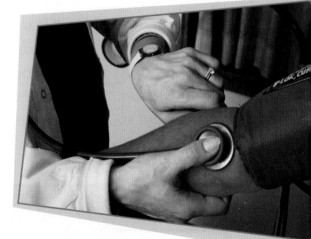

Blood Pressure	Normal	Prehypertension	High
Systolic (mm Hg)	Less than 120	120 to 139	140 or higher
Diastolic (mm Hg)	Less than 80	80 to 89	90 or higher

KNOW YOUR BLOOD CHOLESTEROL LEVELS

Cholesterol is a fatlike substance produced by your liver. The body needs cholesterol, but excess cholesterol can form plaque on the inner wall of your arteries, making it harder for your heart to circulate blood. Over time, plaque can break open and cause blood clots to form. If a clot blocks an artery to the brain, it causes a stroke. If it blocks an artery to the heart, it causes a heart attack.

Among African Americans age 20 and older, nearly 45 percent of men and about 42 percent of women have total blood cholesterol levels of 200 mg/dL or higher. Are you one of them? Get a simple blood test to **find out if your blood cholesterol level is desirable, is borderline-high, or puts you at high risk of developing heart disease and stroke** (see the chart below). Contact your local American Heart Association to find out about free or low-cost screenings in your community.

Talk to your doctor about managing high blood cholesterol. Eating a healthy diet and being more physically active are good ways to start. If your cholesterol stays high, you may need medication to help reduce your risk. Be sure to take your medication as prescribed, and talk to your doctor before you stop taking it.

Cholesterol Level (mg/dL)	Desirable (low risk)	Borderline-High Risk	High Risk
Total cholesterol	Less than 200	200 to 239	240 or higher
LDL ("bad") cholesterol	Less than 130*	130 to 159	160 or higher
HDL ("good") cholesterol	40 or higher for men; 50 or higher for women**	Less than 40 for men; less than 50 for women	Less than 40 for men; less than 50 for women

*People who have had an ischemic stroke or heart attack (or are at risk for having one) may be advised by their doctor to keep their LDL level below 100 or, if they're at very high risk, below 70 mg/dL.

**The higher, the better—an HDL level of 60 mg/dL and above is considered protective against heart disease.

MONITOR FOR DIABETES

Most of the food we eat turns into glucose, or sugar, for our bodies to use for energy. The hormone insulin helps glucose enter the cells of the body. When you have diabetes, your body either doesn't make enough insulin or can't use its own insulin as well as it should, or both. This results in increased blood levels of glucose.

Diabetes is very common in the African American community, but many people don't even know they have it. **Have your glucose (blood sugar) levels checked regularly, especially if you have a family history of diabetes.** People with diabetes often also have high blood pressure and high blood cholesterol and are overweight, further increasing their risk for heart disease and stroke.

A random glucose test (nonfasting) reading of 185 or more or a fasting test reading of 126 or more, measured on at least two occasions, indicates that you may have diabetes. A fasting test reading of 100 to 125 indicates a condition called prediabetes. If your glucose level falls in either category, consult with your doctor to learn how to monitor and prevent or manage diabetes.

Knowledge is **Power.**

Power gives you personal control.

AIM FOR A HEALTHY WEIGHT

Obesity is a major concern for all Americans. You have a much higher risk of heart disease and stroke if you're overweight or obese, even if you have no other risk factors. Excess body fat—especially at your waist—raises blood pressure and blood cholesterol levels and increases your risk of developing diabetes.

You often can decrease your risk of heart disease and stroke by losing as little as 10 to 20 pounds. Establish a sensible eating and exercise plan that will help you reach and maintain a healthy weight. Avoid fad diets and promotions that promise you will lose weight quickly. You don't gain weight overnight, so it makes sense that you can't expect to lose it that way and keep it off for the long term. Obesity is not an appearance issue; it's a health issue. Whether you like the way you look or not, you owe it to yourself to develop a healthy lifestyle.

BE PHYSICALLY ACTIVE

It's well known that being physically active improves your cardiovascular fitness, but you may not realize that consistent inactivity actually increases your risk for heart disease and stroke.

Make your goal at least 30 minutes of physical activity on most days of the week. Being active can help you prevent or control high blood pressure, high blood cholesterol, diabetes, and obesity and overweight. Exercise can also help you reduce stress levels, give you more energy, and improve your self-image. Choose an activity that you enjoy, set reasonable short- and long-term goals, and remember to reward yourself along the way as you achieve your goals.

Make healthy lifestyle choices to manage risk factors such as high blood pressure or diabetes.

LEARN THE WARNING SIGNS AND TAKE THE PLEDGE

Learn to recognize the warning signs of stroke, listed in the pledge below. Acting quickly when these signs occur can make a significant difference in the outcome after a stroke. Share this information with your loved ones to show you care.

Join the Movement!

Show your commitment: Take the pledge. Then copy this page and post it where you will be reminded that you have the power to end stroke.

· ·

As an African American, I pledge...

I'm real. I'm strong. I'm proud. But I'm at risk for stroke. The American Stroke Association is ready to talk to me about what matters—to me. They can meet me where I am—to make positive lifestyle changes. They can make a positive impact—on me and my legacy.

So I pledge...

To not just survive—but thrive. I will learn how to live stronger and longer—for me, my family, and my community. I will join the movement to prevent and overcome stroke.

I will call 9-1-1 immediately if I or someone I know experiences these signs of stroke:

- **Sudden numbness or weakness of the face, arm, or leg, especially on one side of the body**
- **Sudden confusion or trouble speaking or understanding**
- **Sudden trouble seeing in one or both eyes**
- **Sudden trouble walking, dizziness, or loss of balance or coordination**
- **Sudden severe headache with no known cause**

Signature _____ Date _____

Call **1-888-4-STROKE** or visit **StrokeAssociation.org/power** for more information.

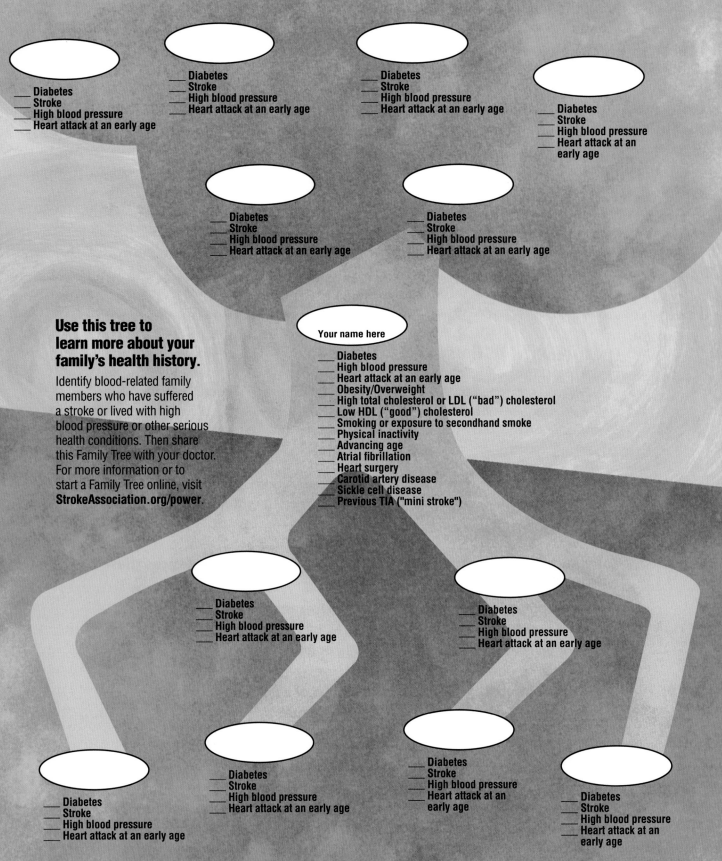

___ Diabetes
___ Stroke
___ High blood pressure
___ Heart attack at an early age

___ Diabetes
___ Stroke
___ High blood pressure
___ Heart attack at an early age

___ Diabetes
___ Stroke
___ High blood pressure
___ Heart attack at an early age

___ Diabetes
___ Stroke
___ High blood pressure
___ Heart attack at an early age

___ Diabetes
___ Stroke
___ High blood pressure
___ Heart attack at an early age

___ Diabetes
___ Stroke
___ High blood pressure
___ Heart attack at an early age

Use this tree to learn more about your family's health history.

Identify blood-related family members who have suffered a stroke or lived with high blood pressure or other serious health conditions. Then share this Family Tree with your doctor. For more information or to start a Family Tree online, visit **StrokeAssociation.org/power**.

Your name here

___ Diabetes
___ High blood pressure
___ Heart attack at an early age
___ Obesity/Overweight
___ High total cholesterol or LDL ("bad") cholesterol
___ Low HDL ("good") cholesterol
___ Smoking or exposure to secondhand smoke
___ Physical inactivity
___ Advancing age
___ Atrial fibrillation
___ Heart surgery
___ Carotid artery disease
___ Sickle cell disease
___ Previous TIA ("mini stroke")

___ Diabetes
___ Stroke
___ High blood pressure
___ Heart attack at an early age

___ Diabetes
___ Stroke
___ High blood pressure
___ Heart attack at an early age

___ Diabetes
___ Stroke
___ High blood pressure
___ Heart attack at an early age

___ Diabetes
___ Stroke
___ High blood pressure
___ Heart attack at an early age

___ Diabetes
___ Stroke
___ High blood pressure
___ Heart attack at an early age

___ Diabetes
___ Stroke
___ High blood pressure
___ Heart attack at an early age

KNOW YOUR RISKS

You don't have to become a statistic! You have the power to reduce your risk of heart disease and stroke. The quiz that follows will help you see where you need to focus your efforts. Then work with your doctor to prevent, reduce, or control as many risk factors as you can.

Check all that apply to you. **If you check two or more, please see your doctor for a complete assessment of your risk.**

AGE
____You are a man over 45 or a woman over 55 years old.

FAMILY HISTORY
____You have a close blood relative who had a heart attack or stroke before age 55 (if father or brother) or before age 65 (if mother or sister).

MEDICAL HISTORY
____You have coronary artery disease or you have had a heart attack.
____You have had a stroke.
____You have an abnormal heartbeat.

Tobacco SMOKE
____You smoke or you live or work with people who smoke every day.

BLOOD PRESSURE
____Your blood pressure is 140/90 mm Hg or higher, or you've been told that your blood pressure is too high.
____You don't know what your blood pressure is.

Total CHOLESTEROL and HDL cholesterol
____Your total cholesterol level is 240 mg/dL or higher.
____Your HDL ("good") cholesterol level is less than 40 mg/dL if you're a man or less than 50 mg/dL if you're a woman.
____You don't know your total cholesterol or HDL levels.

PHYSICAL INACTIVITY
____You don't accumulate at least 30 minutes of physical activity on most days of the week.

Excess BODY WEIGHT
____You are 20 pounds or more overweight.

DIABETES
____You have diabetes or take medicine to control your blood sugar.

Tales From the Heart

Lillian V. Jones-Tubbs

It was a morning like any other workday for Lillian V. Jones-Tubbs, a nursing manager and staff nurse at the MetroHealth System's Broadway Health Center in Cleveland, Ohio. She was standing in her closet, trying to decide what to wear, when her left side suddenly went dead, causing her to fall against the closet door frame and to the floor.

With a shock, she realized that she could not move her left side. Jones-Tubbs remained on the closet floor for about 10 minutes before she felt a little better. Bit by bit, she regained the ability to move her fingers and toes; within about 30 minutes, most of the feeling on her left side also returned.

As frightening as the experience was, Jones-Tubbs did something almost beyond comprehension: She finished getting dressed and went to work, as though nothing had happened. And she went to work every day for the next week without seeking medical help.

As a nurse, Jones-Tubbs had a pretty good idea what had happened in her closet and knew better than most people how dangerous ignoring her symptoms could be. But as a frightened person experiencing those symptoms, she chose denial. She simply did not want to know or to believe that she could be suffering a major stroke.

> She simply did not want to know or to believe that she could be suffering a major stroke.

"After all," she rationalized, "my symptoms got better, so it was probably just TIAs [transient ischemic attacks]. You can have TIAs days, weeks, or months before you have a major stroke. When you have a TIA, a blood clot temporarily interrupts blood flow to the brain, then it dislodges itself and continues on in the body. Some people call TIAs a minor stroke."

After a week at work, where no one noticed the slight weakness on her left side, Jones-Tubbs asked a doctor to take a look at her. She was finally admitted to the hospital, where a series of tests confirmed that she had suffered a full-blown stroke, not the "minor" event that she had self-diagnosed. Doctors also discovered that Jones-Tubbs had a small hole in her heart.

Although she had no history of heart trouble, Jones-Tubbs did have a warning sign: Her blood pressure readings gradually had risen for about a year prior to her stroke, including a series of high blood pressure spikes six months before the event. She was also a smoker, didn't pay much attention to her diet, didn't exercise much, and was 50 pounds overweight.

After her diagnosis, Jones-Tubbs was put on medication and was in physical therapy for a year. The stroke, she says, "left me with a slight droop on the left side of my face that most people don't even notice."

Jones-Tubbs is busier than ever, working two jobs as a family practice nurse. She is 20 pounds lighter, eats a diet low in cholesterol, uses a pedometer to make sure she gets in enough walking, and, of course, no longer smokes.

Before her stroke, Jones-Tubbs didn't go to the doctor very often, even when she was sick. Now she goes regularly. "Nurses and doctors don't make the best patients!" she says. "Now I see my doctor every two to three months and specialists in between. Occasionally I go back to physical therapy when I start getting a little weaker on my left side."

Having learned the hard way that denial and self-diagnosis are not the best courses to follow when dealing with stroke, Jones-Tubbs has the following encouragement for other stroke survivors or those at risk for stroke. "Learn as much as you can about stroke and heart disease, and women's health in general," she says. "Know your family history. If you are a smoker, stop smoking. And be sure to watch what you eat, because you are what you eat."

66 Learn as much as you can about stroke and heart disease.... Know your family history. **99**

Tales From the Heart

Tommie Carlisle, Jr.

Running, golf, racquetball, basketball, swimming—you name it and lifelong fitness buff Tommie Carlisle, Jr., of Mobile, Alabama, did it, hit it, swatted it, threw it, or swam it. At 52 years old, though, the retired military combat medic and physical therapist started to experience occasional dizziness.

He went to his doctor, who suspected vertigo, a condition that causes dizziness, whirling sensations, and sometimes balance problems. A week later, during a round of golf, Carlisle experienced dizziness so severe that he was forced to stop playing. He drove himself home to lie down and relax a bit. " I wasn't worried," he recalls. "I was too active and fit to have anything serious wrong with me. Plus I'd always been blessed with very good health."

On a Sunday afternoon, after returning home from singing in his church choir, Carlisle again felt dizzy, even after lying down. His wife, Mary, suggested that eating something might make him feel better, so Carlisle got up and went to the kitchen for some shrimp Creole.

Suddenly, life as he knew it changed forever. "I became dizzy like no time before," he says. "The house started spinning, I felt nauseous, and I began to sweat profusely. I could no longer stand and had to sit on the floor. I also became disoriented."

At the time of his stroke, Carlisle smoked five to six cigarettes a week.

Luckily for Carlisle, his daughter, Leticia, who was just finishing nursing school, was there and immediately called 9-1-1. Carlisle was admitted to the hospital, where CT and MRI scans confirmed that he had suffered a major stroke.

At the time of his stroke, Carlisle smoked five to six cigarettes a week. Other risk factors included family history: His mother died of a massive stroke at age 46, and his father had hypertension and died from heart disease at 54.

Three years after his stroke, Carlisle credited "six months of rehab and prayer" for a remarkable recovery. He returned to his retirement career in healthcare management at the University of South Alabama in Mobile and added to his family, adopting two boys, ages 10 and 13.

Carlisle is playing golf again, but he's also added more walking to his fitness regimen. Other lifestyle changes include being more cautious about what he eats and how much he eats. "I now read nutrition labels," he says with a note of pride, "and I avoid stress, try to get enough rest, and smile and pray continually."

In addition to rebuilding his life and starting a new family, Carlisle "builds homes and families" with Habitat for Humanity and mentors young kids. "One thing I learned through all of this," he says, "is that it is not about me. It's about who I can help and what I can do for my fellow man."

Carlisle's advice for stroke survivors? "Pray, never get down on yourself, try to smile through all of your trials, and always believe that no matter how things turn out, you're going to be okay in life."

66 I now read nutrition labels and I avoid stress, try to get enough rest, and smile and pray continually. 99

Get Involved

The American Heart Association nationwide education programs help people live healthier, more productive lives. These are just a few of the ways we're fighting cardiovascular disease and stroke. We invite you to join us in that fight. Please call 1-800-AHA-USA1 (1-800-242-8721) or visit americanheart.org for more information on the following programs. For stroke-related information, call 1-888-4-STROKE or visit StrokeAssociation.org.

 **The Heart Of Diabetes: Understanding Insulin Resistance**SM helps people with diabetes take action to reduce their risk for cardiovascular disease. This program helps raise awareness that diabetes dramatically increases a person's risk for heart disease and stroke and often is associated with risk factors such as high blood pressure, cholesterol disorders, obesity, and insulin resistance.

 **Search Your Heart/ Conozca Su Corazón** is a community-based education program that targets heart disease and stroke and provides tools to promote heart-healthy lifestyles to African Americans and Hispanics/Latinos.

 **Choose To Move**SM is a free 12-week program that shows women how to love their bodies by exercising regularly, selecting nutritious foods, and taking time for themselves. Becoming more active and eating well will help women better juggle work, family, and life's other demands.

Look to the **American Heart Association Food Certification Program** for help in selecting heart-healthy foods. The program's heart-check mark is an easy, reliable tool you can use while grocery shopping to quickly identify products that are heart-healthy. For a complete list of certified products, visit heartcheckmark.org. Save more time. Use the free online grocery list builder to create and print a heart-healthy shopping list you can take to the store.

♥ American Heart Association
Meets American Heart Association food criteria for saturated fat and cholesterol for healthy people over age 2.
heartcheckmark.org

 The **American Heart Association Consumer Publications** include a bestselling library of cookbooks and consumer health books. The *American Heart Association Low-Salt Cookbook, Third Edition,* is the perfect guide to learning how to prepare satisfying and healthy meals that are also low in sodium. With more than 200 mouthwatering recipes, this book proves that a low-salt diet is not only good for you but delicious too.

Look for these other American Heart Association cookbooks wherever books are sold:

American Heart Association No-Fad Diet: A Personal Plan for Healthy Weight Loss

The New American Heart Association Cookbook, Seventh Edition

American Heart Association Low-Fat, Low-Cholesterol Cookbook, Third Edition

American Heart Association Low-Calorie Cookbook

American Heart Association Quick & Easy Cookbook

American Heart Association Meals in Minutes Cookbook

American Heart Association One-Dish Meals

Stroke Connection Magazine provides support to stroke survivors and their families with inspiring stories from fellow survivors and caregivers. It also includes practical tips for daily living, information on reducing the risk of another stroke, and news about stroke treatments, research, public policy, and programs. This four-color magazine is published six times a year and is free to individual subscribers. To subscribe call the American Stroke Association at 1-888-4-STROKE or visit StrokeAssociation.org.

RECIPE INDEX

RECIPE INDEX

METRIC CONVERSION CHART

VOLUME MEASUREMENTS (dry)

1/8 teaspoon = 0.5 mL
1/4 teaspoon = 1 mL
1/2 teaspoon = 2 mL
3/4 teaspoon = 4 mL
1 teaspoon = 5 mL
1 tablespoon = 15 mL
2 tablespoons = 30 mL
1/4 cup = 60 mL
1/3 cup = 75 mL
1/2 cup = 125 mL
2/3 cup = 150 mL
3/4 cup = 175 mL
1 cup = 250 mL
2 cups = 1 pint = 500 mL
3 cups = 750 mL
4 cups = 1 quart = 1 L

VOLUME MEASUREMENTS (fluid)

1 fluid ounce (2 tablespoons) = 30 mL
4 fluid ounces (1/2 cup) = 125 mL
8 fluid ounces (1 cup) = 250 mL
12 fluid ounces (1 1/2 cups) = 375 mL
16 fluid ounces (2 cups) = 500 mL

WEIGHTS (mass)

1/2 ounce = 15 g
1 ounce = 30 g
3 ounces = 90 g
4 ounces = 120 g
8 ounces = 225 g
10 ounces = 285 g
12 ounces = 360 g
16 ounces = 1 pound = 450 g

DIMENSIONS

1/16 inch = 2 mm
1/8 inch = 3 mm
1/4 inch = 6 mm
1/2 inch = 1.5 cm
3/4 inch = 2 cm
1 inch = 2.5 cm

OVEN TEMPERATURES

250°F = 120°C
275°F = 140°C
300°F = 150°C
325°F = 160°C
350°F = 180°C
375°F = 190°C
400°F = 200°C
425°F = 220°C
450°F = 230°C

BAKING PAN SIZES

Utensil	Size in Inches/Quarts	Metric Volume	Size in Centimeters
Baking or Cake Pan (square or rectangular)	8×8×2	2 L	20×20×5
	9×9×2	2.5 L	23×23×5
	12×8×2	3 L	30×20×5
	13×9×2	3.5 L	33×23×5
Loaf Pan	8×4×3	1.5 L	20×10×7
	9×5×3	2 L	23×13×7
Round Layer Cake Pan	8×1½	1.2 L	20×4
	9×1½	1.5 L	23×4
Pie Plate	8×1¼	750 mL	20×3
	9×1¼	1 L	23×3
Baking Dish or Casserole	1 quart	1 L	—
	1½ quart	1.5 L	—
	2 quart	2 L	—